Public
Relations

Public
Relations

Angela Murray

TEACH YOURSELF BOOKS

For UK order queries: please contact Bookpoint Ltd, 130 Milton Park, Abingdon, Oxon OX14 4SB. Telephone: (44) 01235 827720. Fax: (44) 01235 400454. Lines are open from 9.00–18.00, Monday to Saturday, with a 24-hour message answering service. Email address: orders@bookpoint.co.uk

For U.S.A. order queries: please contact McGraw-Hill Customer Services, P.O. Box 545, Blacklick, OH 43004-0545, U.S.A. Telephone: 1-800-722-4726. Fax: 1-614-755-5645.

For Canada order queries: please contact McGraw-Hill Ryerson Ltd., 300 Water St, Whitby, Ontario L1N 9B6, Canada. Telephone: 905 430 5000. Fax: 905 430 5020.

Long renowned as the authoritative source for self-guided learning – with more than 30 million copies sold worldwide – the *Teach Yourself* series includes over 300 titles in the fields of languages, crafts, hobbies, business and education.

British Library Cataloguing in Publication Data
A catalogue record for this title is available from The British Library.

Library of Congress Catalog Card Number: On file

First published in UK 2001 by Hodder Headline Plc, 338 Euston Road, London, NW1 3BH.

First published in US 2001 by Contemporary Books, A Division of The McGraw-Hill Companies, 4255 West Touhy Avenue, Lincolnwood (Chicago), Illinois 60712–1975 U.S.A.

The 'Teach Yourself' name and logo are registered trade marks of Hodder & Stoughton Ltd.

Copyright © 2001 Angela Murray

Typeset by Transet Limited, Coventry, England.
Printed in Great Britain for Hodder & Stoughton Educational, a division of Hodder Headline Plc, 338 Euston Road, London NW1 3BH by Cox & Wyman Ltd, Reading, Berkshire.

Impression number   10 9 8 7 6 5 4 3 2 1
Year   2007 2006 2005 2004 2003 2002 2001

CONTENTS

ACKNOWLEDGEMENTS

I would like to thank the following for their invaluable assistance: Chris Lowe, Head of Public Affairs for PricewaterhouseCoopers and Membership Secretary of the IPR Government Affairs Group, for information on Government affairs and lobbying, Chapter 9; Neil Mainland, Partner at Financial Dynamics and Deputy Chairman of the IPR City and Financial Group, for information on financial PR, also Chapter 9; and Richard Hubbard, former journalist and now Assistant Director, Sales and Marketing, Cambridge International Examinations (part of the University of Cambridge) for comments and advice on dealing with the media, Chapter 3. And to HarperCollins Publishers for permission to use the dictionary definition given on page 1.

I would also like to give special thanks to my family, especially to Anna and Sarah.

1 | **INTRODUCTION**

Everyone 'does' PR it seems – but what exactly do they do?

This book is written for anyone who (a) knows they should be using PR as part of their marketing strategy but (b) is not sure exactly what it is or (c) how they should evaluate its worth. You probably run, or are a member of, a marketing team within a small or medium sized organization. Or you may be on the management team, or run your own company – but whatever your role you suspect that you should be using PR more proactively. Perhaps you are already 'doing' PR without really trying – you're receiving press coverage for example – and you know you could be making more of the opportunities on offer. Or perhaps your competitors, or other organizations or individuals just like yourself are starting to generate the sort of attention which you know you are equally worthy of.

This book will help unravel the mysteries of PR and help you understand what it's all about, what techniques will suit your organization best, and show you how to assess the performance of your PR campaign.

But let's start at the beginning.

What is PR?

Books such as this often begin by quoting a dictionary definition – and as PR is a term which often proves easy to say, yet hard to explain, it's as good a way of starting as any. So, what does *Collins English Dictionary* say?:

> **public relations** n 1.a the practice of creating, promoting or maintaining goodwill and a favourable image among the public towards an institution, public body, etc.

As this book unfolds you will see that concepts such as 'goodwill' and 'public' are key terms which can be defined in many different ways, but they are nevertheless fundamental to an understanding of what PR actually is. In a nutshell, PR can be used to the benefit of almost every aspect of your organization. It can systemize, develop and improve every conceivable way in which you communicate with those 'publics' most important to you – whether they are customers, clients, investors, suppliers, staff or any other interested groups. Some organizations employ sizeable teams of both in-house and external PR professionals to run their campaigns 24 hours a day, seven days a week – but as this book will demonstrate, in most cases this simply isn't necessary. It may be that you only have to dip into your PR file once or twice a year, when you've got something important to promote, or that you can set up a few PR activities which will then run themselves happily, needing only regular, low-key input. Once you've worked your way through this book, it will be clear as to what is needed in order to make PR work for you.

Let's start by answering a few fundamental questions, in order to help you understand the reasoning behind PR, and to help you to start planning your own campaign.

Why practice Public Relations?

It's rather ironic that PR – the art of promoting a favourable impression – has itself gained quite a poor reputation: it's expensive, it's superficial, it tries to fool a gullible public, and it yields results which are impossible to evaluate. Yet almost every major organization, and an increasing number of SMO's, commit a significant budget to PR year after year – why do they do this?

The benefits of good PR

PR can deliver an enormous range of benefits, and it's important to be aware, at a global level, of what can be achieved in order to enable you to plan a strategy that meets the needs of *your* organization:

Effective, consistent, sustained communication

PR is the art of communication – whether via an appropriate vehicle or 'medium' (such as the media, a web site or literature), or face to face at an exhibition, seminar or other event. A PR strategy will ensure that you are exploiting all possible channels of communication as efficiently as possible – that you are making the most of available opportunities; that you are making sure your messages are clear and relevant; and that your communications are consistent across the board. This will not only ensure that the right people know about your organization, but that the image you present is consistent and coherent, improving recognition and credibility. PR is driven by a full appreciation of the ways in which an audience gains information, using this knowledge as the main inspiration for planning campaign activities.

A versatile marketing tool

PR is both versatile and creative, and encourages the use of a wide range of methods (or 'mechanisms') in order to get a message across to a target audience, and to get it across in the most efficient way possible.

Maintaining ongoing interest in and a better understanding of your organization

PR aims to encourage sustained interest in your organization. By supplying your target audiences with regular information delivered in a variety of ways you can maintain awareness even when you have little new information to promote. This can prove particularly valuable if you are dependent upon high-value, but infrequent sales or contracts. If the window of opportunity is so small, then you must ensure that your market exposure is continuous so that your name will be recognized when the time to make a decision has arrived.

PR can also be used to exploit the knowledge and expertise of your staff, enabling you to generate a better understanding of your organization, its ethos and its ambitions.

Maintaining goodwill

A proven commitment to keeping audiences fully informed can reap valuable rewards, especially in terms of 'goodwill'. And an organization which is not afraid to communicate during bad times as well as good can engender considerable loyalty from those most important to its ongoing success. Effective communications during less successful periods also help stifle rumour and misinformation.

Maximizing investment in other marketing activities

PR is an ideal complement to a host of other marketing initiatives, from advertising to exhibitions. It can also provide more sustained promotion of a particular marketing message, providing a platform on which other activities can ride, and making the most of the overall marketing budget.

Improving staff morale

Positive messages about one's employer can only reinforce a feeling of well-being at work – as long as the messages are accurate of course. Good PR can impact upon staff recruitment and retention, as you find that the quality of candidates for new positions improves as the reputation of your organization is enhanced.

A positive contribution to business success

A 'favourable' image is an invaluable asset. It will encourage loyalty through bad times as well as good, and not just among customers or clients: from employees (current and potential); from financial backers, from the bank manager to shareholders; from your local community (very important if what you do has a direct impact upon their everyday lives or their environment). Of course, customers and clients are vital, as are those who might recommend your company to someone else – they all need to think well of you, to want you to succeed and to want to support you with their time or their money.

The value of 'corporate branding' is becoming increasingly widely appreciated – using PR to promote your organization as a whole as well as the products or services it promotes. PR can help promote core values such as reliability, integrity or innovation that then become associated with every specific promotion that you undertake.

What 'type' of campaign?

PR campaigns fall – very roughly – into a number of broad categories, and it's important that you appreciate the differences between them before deciding which would best suit your own organization. Remember, these categories are not mutually exclusive – most organizations run one or two campaign types in parallel, in order to meet all their objectives:

Trade

You promote your products or services primarily to other businesses – the 'trade' – even though the end-user may be the consumer. A trade campaign tends to be highly targeted and operates within well-defined fields; it frequently runs in conjunction with a consumer campaign (see below) in order to achieve a 'push and pull' effect – encouraging retailers to stock your products for example, whilst also persuading consumers to go and buy them. Trade campaigns tend to focus on a narrower range of communications media – each industry has its own core trade press for example, or key trade exhibitions, and so the PR campaign can be geared to exploit these to full effect. Trade PR can also explore the possibilities offered by 'vertical markets' – markets not directly associated with your product or service but important to the audiences which you wish to influence.

Business to business

Similar in many ways to a trade campaign, business to business PR usually describes the promotion of professional service providers – lawyers, bankers, accountants, business advisers and so on. Business to business campaigns often focus more on the demonstration of knowledge and expertise than the direct promotion of specific products or services. Many campaigns have a strong regional bias, as target audiences tend to be within the local business community, and as a result many national organizations run both local and national campaigns in order to target their audience more effectively.

Consumer

This term is generally applied to any campaign aimed at 'the general public', but in fact, the public is usually closely defined according to a varying set of parameters including age, sex, location, income – the list can be long and sophisticated. Most consumer campaigns demand greater resources as audiences can be very large, the variety of communication channels greater, and more creativity required in order to both attract attention and counter the activities of the competition in what could be a very crowded marketplace.

Corporate

As has already been mentioned, PR can also be used to maintain the reputation of your organization at a 'corporate' level, and corporate campaigns often run alongside other PR programmes to underline core values, and to provide a way of communicating general business information which is of interest to a wider range of audiences. 'Government' or 'Public affairs' campaigns fall within this remit, using PR to enable the effective lobbying of key Government influencers (see Chapter 9 for more on these two specialist areas).

Issue/information

Not all PR campaigns are driven by commercial incentives. PR is just as effective in educating or informing a target audience about a new development, or raising awareness of an issue of concern to audiences of all types and from all sections of the community. PR can prove very effective in educational campaigns as it comprises a range of activities capable of disseminating quite complex or involved information to both very specific and wide-ranging target audiences.

A note on the exercises in this book

At the end of each chapter you'll find a brief exercise, designed to test your understanding of the preceding information, and to help you create, step by step, your own PR programme by completing a 'PR matrix'. This is a simple framework which will allow you to define and link all the various elements of a campaign to ensure that every activity is there for a purpose, and that no aims or objectives have been overlooked. As you work your way through this book, you'll learn about all the activities which could be employed within a PR campaign – if you decide that some of those suggested simply don't suit the nature of your organization, then of course don't include them in your final programme. But even so it's good to know about all the techniques you could use, in case your organization – or your job – changes in the future!

2 PLANNING A PR CAMPAIGN

You may think that the term 'PR campaign' is rather grand for what you had in mind – perhaps a bit of press coverage in the local paper, or a seminar or party for your clients or customers – but whatever your immediate ambitions, gathering your ideas together under the umbrella of a 'campaign' is a sensible way to begin. As with any other marketing activity, strategic forethought is vital. PR can take up a lot of your time and often your money, and if it's not targeted precisely, timed effectively and executed efficiently then all your hard work and valuable budget may go to waste. Don't try and sketch out ideas 'when you've got a minute'. Sit down properly, with colleagues if you think it will help, and work through the stages outlined in this chapter. Don't forget that planning will remain a fairly fluid process for quite a long time – you'll find that the simple exercise of working through your thoughts may make you think again about certain fundamental issues, but as a result you should have a much clearer idea of what you want to do, why you'll be doing it and what the outcome should be. In effect, you'll have created the bones of your 'campaign'.

A note on product and service PR

Although there are many similarities, it's important to highlight the differences between PR campaigns for products and services, and to keep these in mind when starting to plan your own PR strategy.

The essential difference is tangibility. A product is there – it will be visible on a shelf, it can be photographed, it can be seen in action, its benefits can be immediately appreciated. A service does not exist until it is being executed, and therefore the invaluable tangibility has to be created in other ways.

PR is a very useful tool for the service industry, and it can be used to promote services just as effectively as products. Products tend to rise or fall on their own merits, and on the buzz which surrounds them. The importance of the manufacturer is often less to the fore, unless the name brings kudos (i.e. any designer product) or is an important part of the whole package. There are many books on product marketing which go into strategic issues in greater detail than is necessary here.

For a service company, the organization *is* the service – think of any bank or other high street service organization such as a travel agent or accountants – and so target audiences are far more aware of an organization's reputation and history, and this affects their buying patterns and loyalties. Although services can be marketed as 'products' corporate PR plays a much more important role in any campaign for a service organization.

Defining aims and objectives

When putting together any sort of marketing plan, it's important to try and define your aims and objectives right from the start – for the purpose of this book the following definitions are used:

- **Aims** – measurable ambitions
- **Objectives** – the means by which you will achieve your aims

To take a very broad example, the reason why you're reading this book can probably be translated into the following aim:

- To raise the profile of my organization

Which can then be translated into the following objective:

- To put in place a PR campaign

Your marketing plan will have already established the overall marketing aims for your organization, and these will form the basis for your PR campaign. But make sure you don't just use PR as a dumping ground for the corporate wish-list. Keep your PR aims well defined, achievable, and realistic – and this last point may demand some brute honesty about your organization or your product or service. You may think your company is the most fascinating, dynamic organization in the country and that the national press would just love to hear about you – but would they really? Is your organization *that* unusual? Are your products really *that* unique? It's not that you should undersell yourself, but PR is an activity which demands truth (despite what you may have heard), and creating unreasonable, unsustainable hype will not do you any favours in the long run.

Also make sure that the aims you establish are measurable (in some form or another), otherwise, how else can you evaluate them? It's easy to say that your aim is 'to become the best-known design agency in Newcastle', or 'to become leaders in the field of brewing technology', but such statements come apart very quickly under scrutiny. How would you define 'best-known' for example? What exactly is a 'leader in the field'? How can you find out when you've become the 'best-known' or the 'leader'?

Your aims and objectives will also establish the practical parameters of your campaign, the geographical scope for example, timescale and other such factors. It's also very important to remember that PR cannot achieve all your marketing ambitions for you. It will be working in tandem with a number of other marketing activities which will – together – help you to achieve your corporate ambitions. Therefore, tease out those results which PR can realistically hope to accomplish.

Let's consider an example, in order to put these thoughts into perspective.

Klippit is a growing company, which manufactures a revolutionary new re-usable staple, destined – the MD is sure – to revolutionise the lives of office staff everywhere. Having drafted a marketing strategy, the Marketing Director has jotted down the aims which he hopes his PR campaign will achieve:

- ■ *To let everyone know about the Klippit system.*
- ■ *To make Klippit the 'number one' brand of paper fastener.*

Examined closely, these aims are rather breathtaking – to let *everyone* know? Everyone in the country, or in the whole world? And to make Klippit the 'number one' brand – what market share would they need in order to achieve this? How many Klippit units would they have to sell? Do they even manufacture this amount? How quickly would they have to grow in order to realize this ambition? How long are we talking about in order to achieve this – a year? A decade? And how do we know when it's happened?

Admittedly, these are only first thoughts, but it does save time if you can apply more discipline to the process right from the start. So let's see if we can re-draft these thoughts into more realistic PR aims – for example:

- **To promote the Klippit system to our main target customer groups in selected countries – those identified as having maximum potential for growth**
- **To contribute towards a growth rate of 10% per year for worldwide sales, in order to gain 20% of the paper fastener market within 10 years**

As you can see, the aims are now anchored to some practical facts and figures – and although, no doubt, these will be revisited and probably revised as time passes, at least we have a strategic direction in which to go. The sales team have also attached some hard figures to the aim of becoming 'number one' – they've decided, realistically, how much of the existing market they can hope to penetrate, given manufacturing capacity and staffing levels, and defined a timescale in which to achieve that goal. Using terms such as 'contribute' is also practical – as we've already noted, PR will be one of the many tools used to achieve such global aims, and it's important to acknowledge this up front.

Objectives, as we said earlier, are the practical means by which you will achieve your aims, and at this stage it's only necessary to sketch in the broadest possible detail, once again in order to give strategic direction for the next stage of the planning process. So in response to the aims, the objectives can be defined as:

- **To establish a PR campaign which will:**
  - **Raise awareness, at the international level, of both the Klippets organization and of the Klippits brand.**
  - **Educate potential users about the new system.**
  - **Generate quality leads.**

These key objectives define the main campaign drivers: that there are a number of groups of people which need to know about the Klippit system; that these can be defined geographically; and that there is an educational as well as a selling job to be done.

Defining your target audience

Now that you have outlined your aims and objectives – why and how you want to use PR – you can start to consider your target audiences, the people with whom you want to communicate.

Who is most important to your success? Think carefully, because this list could stretch well beyond current and potential customers. Consider the following groups and identify those of most relevance to you – and don't forget to define criteria such as geographical spread or industry sector for each different group:

Customers or clients

This category is probably top of most lists, but rather than being lumped together as one homogenous group, consider sub-dividing them further into former, current and potential customers, as you may need a different strategy for each. For example, former customers need to know about new products or services which could entice them back; helping to maintain the loyalty of existing clients may be an important issue; and how can you convert a potential into a current customer?

If you are launching a consumer campaign, then you need to closely define your customers or clients in order to enable activities to be planned efficiently, as consumer audiences can range enormously in size and characteristics. When planning a trade campaign, as well as identifying the type of client or customer you want to target (probably in the broad terms of their business or activity) it's also important to identify more precisely those job functions within each target organization which are most important to you, and these will probably be at a number of levels. Although your service or product may be desired on the shop floor, for example, it might be the Finance Director who needs to be convinced to spend the money. Likewise, your product may be designed to help a specific team within a company, but the credibility of your organization may need to be proven to the Board of Directors first before your solution is adopted.

'Interested groups'

If you are using PR to promote an issue – rather than to develop a business or service – then you'll need to identify the type of people that you need to target, grouping them by those criteria which will help focus your campaign activities – by location, for example, income, sex, association with a particular event. Look at the ideas for clients and customers as many them are also relevant here. Who is already interested? How can you keep them up to speed? Who has lost interest – can you get them back on board? Who should be informed but isn't?

Distributors or agents

This refers to anyone selling your products or services on your behalf, or using your products to sell their own (using your components to make larger products, for example). If you don't sell directly to your customers then you need to ensure that whoever does is both the target of and supported by your PR campaign, in order to encourage and help them to work harder on your behalf. Direct promotion of your products or services will also improve market conditions for your distributors, and may even increase competition between those distributors who actively want to represent you.

Suppliers

Add these to your list if you are heavily dependent upon their goodwill and support through bad times as well as good. Being perceived as a good customer, especially if your business is clearly growing successfully, will also result in fiercer competition for your business.

Influencers and advisers

This term embraces anyone who may recommend your organization to other target audiences on your list. The nature of the individuals within this group is often quite specific to a particular business. For example, speaking from my own experience, PR consultants are often recommended by designers, advertising agencies and marketing agencies, and also by business advisers – government-funded business agencies, for example, banks or even accountants. In other professions, trade associations can be very influential, or associated or complementary organizations. Think laterally and you may discover that this target audience is more extensive than you think, and also very important.

Financial sector

Even the smallest business needs financial support of some kind, and good PR can help reassure your backers that you are really doing well and deserve ongoing support. As an organization grows, it may need to attract additional funding, so investors or shareholders should be added to the list in due course.

The local community

If your organization operates purely on a local level then this is obviously a key audience, but using PR to maintain a good relationship with your local community can be beneficial in other ways. It can help attract a better quality of staff, for example, and if your organization has a physical impact upon the local environment – perhaps you operate a manufacturing plant, or have a large site within a town – then this becomes even more important, especially if you have plans to expand.

Your staff

We look at internal PR in more detail in Chapter 7, but suffice to say that your staff should not be neglected when planning your PR campaign. Informed staff feel valued and respected, and a robust system of communication also keeps the effects of a damaging rumour-mill to a minimum.

So try to be creative when listing your audiences – once again, think laterally and use as broad a brush as possible. This is the list, jotted down in no particular order, that the Klippit team has come up with:

- *Office workers*
- *PAs/secretaries/admin teams*
- *Office managers – department heads*
- *Home office – teleworkers/self-employed/leisure*
- *Stationery suppliers (shops, catalogues)*
- *Gift shops?*
- *Schools/colleges – students*
- *Bank/Accountant*
- *Klippit reps*
- *Staff*

Let's take another example, this time looking at a service-based organization. The Clean Sweeps provide contract cleaning services to both private homes and offices in and around a small town, targeting anyone who needs a regular cleaner, or a one-off blitz. Not only do they want to expand their portfolio of regular clients, but they also need to constantly recruit cleaners for their books – in fact keeping cleaners is a problem they want to try and address, and so they've made this one of their main aims. Target audiences in this case have been defined and divided as follows:

Customers

- Busy home-owners (i.e. working full-time)
- House-movers
- Office managers
- Landlords/estate agents

Advisers

- Local business advisers (i.e. Chambers of Commerce)
- Other cleaning services (i.e. window cleaning/ ground maintenance)

Staff

- Local people looking for part-time employment
- Job centres and employment advisers
- Existing staff

As you can see, although it's easy to think that you should only try and attract the attention of your customer, there are a whole range of audiences vital to the ongoing success of your organization and your PR campaign should make sure that communications are maintained with every relevant group.

Audience, message and medium

Now that you know to whom you want to talk, the next stage is to decide what to say – the message – and to identify the best way of saying it – the medium.

Messages

Messages are exactly that. The translation of your aims and objectives into messages specific to each individual audience, which they will understand and to which you hope they will respond appropriately. Defining the 'message' is not supposed to be an exercise in 'spin', designed to distort or hide reality but more a means of establishing 'what does this person need to know, what do I want this person to know, and how should I tell him?'.

Let's look at an example, once again from the Klippit campaign. The Klippit team sees 'the secretary' as a key target group, and wants to persuade the secretary to adopt the Klippit system. Messages for this audience will of course include the more obvious, such as:

- 'Klippit is a system which will really benefit my working life', and
- 'Klippit is a much improved alternative to traditional staples because ...'

But PR also encourages the promotion of more subtle messages such as:

- 'Klippit is a growing company which has an exciting future – if my whole office changes to Klippits, then I will still be able to use the system in 10 years time.'

Here are some more examples. Klippits are going to be sold primarily through stationery shops, and so retailers are a prime target. Messages will therefore range from:

to:

■ Klippits is an exciting new brand of paper fastener

to:

■ Customers choosing Klippits will return to me for top-up supplies thus generating extra business

■ Klippits will be backed by an extensive advertising campaign, ensuring my stock will sell fast.

The Clean Sweeps have identified recruitment as a key problem area, so they have decided that their PR programme must include the following messages wherever possible:

■ Clean Sweeps is a good employer, with a good reputation.

■ Clean Sweeps offers services of the highest quality – only the best cleaning staff are employed.

Go through all your audience groups one by one and list all the key messages which you need to get across – you'll probably find that many are common to a number groups, especially those which focus on your organization rather than on a specific product or service, so your final list will be more manageable than you may initially fear.

Remember that although messages are essentially substantive – providing the text or sub-text for an actual activity – they can also act as strategic guidelines, helping you to decide which activities to pursue (which we look at in more detail in the following section). For example, the Clean Sweeps have listed 'We are an excellent local employer' as one of their messages. If they can publicize any good stories about recruitment – perhaps that they've just employed 20 new cleaners for example – then such news is an ideal vehicle for the message they have identified. However, if they were invited to speak on the problems of recruitment at a national employers conference, tempting though the offer might be, they should perhaps turn it down. The conference audience would not be local, would be very unlikely to become a Clean Sweeps client or cleaner, and the emphasis is on a problem rather than success – the opposite of their defined message.

Medium/activity

The medium – or activity – is the method you choose of getting each message across to the target audience. PR is primarily thought of as a press-based activity – using the media to publicize your news – and 'media liaison' is still very much the bread and butter of many PR campaigns. But PR encourages versatility, and there are many other ways of getting a message across, as you will discover as you work your way through the rest of this book.

It's important to keep in mind the fundamental nature of each audience when considering this element of campaign planning. What are the main characteristics of this group – are they geographically widespread for example, or concentrated locally? Are they a small group or do they number in thousands? And – most important of all –what are the most effective means of communication when talking to this target group?

If your audience is geographically widespread, and numerically potentially unlimited (as for, say a consumer campaign for chocolate), then a wide-ranging media campaign may well be a good way to start, in order to achieve extensive nationwide coverage. But if your audience is either very small or very discrete, and your message very specific or complex then a media campaign may too broad-brush, too transitory or too superficial, to have the desired effect. A seminar or social event may be more effective, or a directly mailed newsletter may be a more cost-effective means of achieving the desired result.

The PR audit

Most organizations don't start their PR plan with a clean sheet. They've already been practising PR, perhaps in an ad hoc way, for many years or they have already gained some publicity without really trying, perhaps because they have grown spectacularly quickly. If you are such an organization, (but even if you're not) then it may be worth implementing a PR audit right at the start of your campaign.

A PR audit is a way of finding out exactly what your ad hoc (and other, more sustained) PR activities have achieved in terms of your reputation, awareness of products or services, and your ranking against competitors or other similar organizations. PR audits are also useful for those organizations who wish to ramp up their PR programme, and want guidance on the best direction in which to go, or for those who feel their PR has stagnated, and need to know why.

PR audits tend to be qualitative rather than quantitative pieces of research: in other words, rather than questioning large numbers of relevant people (your customers for example), fewer, but more influential or representative individuals are targeted and usually asked more in-depth questions. For example, an influential journalist on a key trade paper could give very interesting insights on your reputation within the media; a management consultant may also be able to speak for a great number of clients on issues such as reputation and standing.

In a perfect world, the audit should be carried out before a PR campaign has been launched and then repeated after it has been completed or has been running for a set period of time. But in reality few organizations have the budget to carry out such research on a regular basis – and the impact of a PR campaign can be measured reasonably effectively in other ways (see Chapter 11). But even if an audit is only carried out once in a blue moon, it can still provide invaluable reassurance that the PR programme is on track, or that certain audiences need to be addressed in a different way, and it will also give a unique snapshot of the marketplace in which your PR programme has to be effective.

If you plan to undergo such an exercise, keep your questionnaire as short and to the point as possible, and suitable for a telephone interview. You can either reveal your organization's name at the beginning, the middle or at the end of the exercise – if you are already quite well known then hiding behind anonymity for at least part of the interview may help increase the honesty of the answers you receive. If you are relatively unknown, then you'll lose nothing by identifying yourselves up front. Most audits go for a half and half approach – asking general questions first, then identifying the originator of the audit before moving on to more specific questions about reputation and so on.

When thinking about your questionnaire, make sure you address issues such as the most widely respected media (press, broadcast, internet) for each audience; the way target groups gain different types of information; the reputation of your organization (couched in terms relevant and meaningful to your aims i.e. reliable, honest, fast-growing, fly-by-night), and the way you are perceived when compared to other organizations, both competitor and complementary. Specific questions will depend greatly upon the nature of your target audiences and the status you have already gained. Your main aim is to gain a picture of what PR has achieved for you so far, and where the best opportunities now lie.

Ideally you should get professional help when drafting your questionnaire, and even to implement to survey itself. Telephone interviews – even when the target list is reasonably limited – can prove very time consuming, and you'll want to complete the exercise in as short a timescale as possible in order to gather an accurate snapshot of the situation at a particular time. Market research specialists and PR professionals will both be able to help. Of course, you will still have to provide a list of contacts to interview, drawn from each of your target audiences. Try to generate a list comprising both those who you know are familiar with your organization and those totally unknown to you, in order to get a good end result.

If your budget is restricted, or the questions you've identified are quite limited, then you may be able to tack the audit onto the back of another market research exercise – even if it's just a case of adding a few quick questions to a customer satisfaction form.

Timing

When is the best time to launch your campaign? Is the season important (as it is in the agricultural, health or gardening industries)? Is there a major industry event, such as a trade fair, which would provide a good focus for your campaign launch, or would you in fact prefer to wait until the show is over and everyone is looking for something new? Do your clients have well-known financial markers – say a common end of year – which may result in higher or lower spending? Are January and September the best dates (these are frequently cited as good times of year, being the return from major holiday periods)? How does your timing translate overseas, if your audiences are spread around the globe?

The timing of each individual PR activity is also important – some will need to be regular in order to maintain impact (the generation of press coverage for example, or the issue of a newsletter). Some activities will work better as a one-off (special events for example), and others are designed specifically to deliver more sustained results, such as a sponsorship programme. Once you have identified the most important regular dates in your PR calendar, then make sure your additional activities – if you have any left! – are evenly spaced throughout the rest of the year, in order to maintain an even flow of information going out to your target groups, and also to avoid stressing your PR team too much! For example, some will be seasonal (outdoor events, or those linked to a specific holiday); some will have to tie in with the calendar of the target audience (to focus on a particular trade exhibition etc.); some may take advantage of an external initiative – a national campaign day for example. Activities also have specific lead times, and these need to be appreciated well in advance, if deadlines – and opportunities – are not to be missed.

A final point – the timing of your campaign will also influence the nature of the PR team which you put together (see the next section, and Chapter 10, for more on this). If you know that you'll only ever be doing one or two main activities a year, then you can create a flexible team comprising part-time in-house and external help. If the campaign is to be long-term and sustained, then the creation of a dedicated team, or the employment of a full-time PRO (Public Relations Officer) is more logical, and will also underline the commitment to PR that you, as an organization, is making.

Managing a PR campaign

You may have pinned down your audiences, refined your messages and identified a range of activities, but there are still some important details – both strategic and administrative – to be put in place before you can start.

Staff and resources

If PR remains constantly at the bottom of your list of things to do, then it will never be effective or deliver real results. You'll always be reacting to events, never making the most of upcoming opportunities, and constantly feel that things could be handled better – especially when you see what your competitors have achieved. Good PR is a balance of pro- and reactive activities and so your PR campaign, and the resources supporting it, should be capable of managing both.

PR needs dedicated time, both for planning and for implementation, and the amount of time needed depends, of course, on the scope of your plans. Once you have decided on the PR activities that will best achieve your aims you can then estimate how much time will be needed to fulfil your ambitions, and plan your staffing arrangements accordingly.

When it comes to running a PR campaign, there are a number of options: using in-house personnel, either full or part time; employing a PR agency or freelance consultant; or using a mixture of the two. In Chapter 10 we look in more detail at the dynamics of a PR team, and also at what PR professionals can offer and how they should be used. Remember, you'll probably need assistance on two levels – strategic and administrative. Despite the excellent advice given in this book, you probably need specialist help at some level to help you steer your campaign through its first few months using either a consultant, or exploiting in-house expertise on a formal basis. Depending on the activity, PR can also be highly labour intensive so make sure you have someone on the PR team able to handle database management, envelop stuffing and record keeping. If you are planning any sort of major event, you'll also need to identify willing hands able to help out when needed.

Ongoing review and evaluation

Once again, this topic has been given a chapter to itself, but it deserves to be mentioned here because it will influence the way you set up and run your PR campaign.

As your campaign proceeds, you should be constantly reviewing and re-evaluating the essential elements which are in play – and Chapter 11 demonstrates how this can be done. Practically, this demands that the PR team meets at appropriate intervals to both review what's going on, evaluate results, and to brainstorm new ideas. Regular meetings also allow you to consider new opportunities which have arisen since you started planning your campaign – or new threats. PR should always remain a flexible resource; there will always be set activities which will dominate your PR strategy – major trade exhibitions for example, or product launches – but around these, you should attempt to be as proactive as possible. Brainstorming sessions are also an opportunity for other members of your organization to get involved. They may not understand the mechanics of PR, but they may still be able to provide new ideas and angles on what can be done, and identify new opportunities. It's also important to remember that PR is a service for the organization as a whole, and should remain responsive to the needs of *all* employees.

Exercise

A new 'Organic Centre' is being set up in a local town. It hopes to provide information on all aspects of the organic movement, and will sell organic produce both in its shop and its own café. It also hopes to act as a catalyst for changing public and national opinion. The Centre managers are now beginning to sketch out a PR programme. What are the Centre's PR aims, and how can they be translated into realistic objectives? Which target audiences should they list? And what do they want to say to each?

PR Matrix

You could sketch out your answers to the question above by starting a PR Matrix – and then start to draft one for your own organization. Your first actions is, of course, to establish your aims and objectives and then complete the first two columns of your matrix, heading these 'target audience' and 'main messages', making sure that there are no gaps. If your aims are wide ranging then you may find that you have to create a number of different matrices and develop discrete programmes, but make sure they are integrated into the overall campaign.

3 | MEDIA LIAISON

'Media liaison' often plays the leading role within a PR programme (both in its own right, and in support of other activities), and may in fact be the only activity that an organization wants to implement. The term is used to describe the structured approach to gaining relevant, quality coverage in the media – print, broadcast and electronic. It embraces both the proactive – issuing press releases and so on – and the reactive, and although the focus of such a campaign is usually the promotion of stories about your organization, media coverage can also be given to events and other activities specially created to generate 'news'.

A media campaign has to be planned meticulously, and sustained over the long term if good results are to be achieved. The press will rarely come rushing to your door unless you have something absolutely staggering to say, and so you have to be the one who creates the opportunities. A lot of time and energy can be spent trying to gain media coverage, with little to show for it at the end. This chapter explains how to start planning your press campaign, and how to make sure you maximize your chances of success.

The ultimate goal is to gain good exposure in the right vehicle, even though this cannot always be guaranteed – and strategies must also be put in place to deal with any negative coverage you might receive. The breadth of your media liaison programme depends greatly upon the size of your organization, and upon the quality and nature of the information you can supply. Of course, the bigger or more influential you are, the more you become news in your own right, and therefore have to be prepared to monitor, analyse and respond to coverage on an almost daily basis.

For the vast majority of organizations, media liaison is mainly proactive, undertaken because media coverage is often considered to be very important, especially if one's main rival has just been featured in a key publication! A good feature in an important magazine, for example, is often considered as an independent, informed endorsement of your product or organization and can carry a value that far exceeds the results of any other type of marketing activity.

Identifying your target media

Your first job is to identify the media in which you would like to gain coverage. Look back at your list of target audiences and work from there, thinking of the type of media each audience would read, watch or listen to. Don't try to be too specific at this stage – we're simply trying to identify some basic categories – and once again, think creatively and as broadly as possible.

Listed below are some of the most easily identifiable categories to get you started, and ways of refining these categories further. Remember that you don't have to include all these categories on your press list, tempting though it might be – only choose those which you know cover stories relevant to the activities of your organization, and which, of course, are read by your target audiences. You can always expand the list on an ad hoc basis if you suddenly have a story which you know is of wider interest. The structure of your list also depends upon the geographical scope of your campaign. At the moment, we're really only dealing with 'domestic' media – you may have to repeat the exercise country by country if you are planning a major international campaign.

So, consider the following:

- **National daily and weekly newspapers and news magazines:** consider which correspondents are most relevant (i.e. science and technology, lifestyle, business) or if you only want to contact the newsdesk; you could also get lists of local 'stringers' – journalists based in your area who pick up on stories and forward them to the national media.
- **National and local radio and TV:** identify those programmes which may pick up on your news, or which will be interested more generally in your

organization and what it does (feature programmes, special interest programmes etc.); if you want to target newsdesks, then once again try to identify the most relevant correspondent; and identify local stringers who can work on your behalf.

TV is a rapidly expanding sector, due to new developments in satellite, digital and interactive broadcasting, and the boundaries between the different types of media are beginning to blur. However, despite the proliferation of new channels and programmes, and the seemingly insatiable desire for content, audience numbers have not increased so rapidly. The same number of viewers will simply be shared out more thinly between the programmes now being shown, so when assessing broadcast options, especially if you only have limited resources, simply pick the most popular programmes – which will probably be those that you knew about already!

- **Regional daily and weekly newspapers (including freesheets):** regional publications number in their hundreds, so if you plan to target them, break down your selection by specific region or by circulation (to identify the most widely read publications in each area) in order to generate a more manageable list.

- **Web-based publications:** once again, identify the most appropriate correspondents, and check that the subscription profile matches that of your target audiences.

- **Online news services and news agencies:** these are primarily news-based services, feeding journalists on daily and weekly national and regional media, so only include them if you plan to issue highly topical news stories with widespread appeal or interest. Regional news services also exist, and these may be worth researching in more depth, especially if they are keen to promote organizations within their area.

- **Consumer publications:** this term refers to those publications aimed at the 'general public', including general interest titles (i.e. 'lifestyle', women's magazines) and the more specific (such as sport, food or hobby magazines), for all age groups and for all stages of life. As you will already know from your own experience, consumer titles proliferate, and can come and go very quickly and so this category needs regular review if it is important to your overall strategy.

- **Industry-specific trade publications:** every industry has at least one or two publications which are read by everyone, and many are well known outside their industry. You need to identify the key publications for each industry sector you wish to target – ask some members of your target audiences to provide guidelines. Circulation numbers can provide another indicator, but only up to a certain point. Some subscription-only publications, with quite a limited circulation, can prove to be the most influential.

- **General business publications:** certain business publications – especially those aimed at management level staff – are read across all industry sectors, and can be very influential. Regional business magazines and newspapers can also be well read, and can prove useful if you are marketing at a regional level. However, they usually only cover news about organizations local to their area, so only contact those outside your own region if you can demonstrate a strong local connection.

- **Association newsletters and magazines (both professional and amateur):** most professional organizations (trade associations or professional bodies) publish their own newsletters and magazines, many very influential in their own right, and so should be included if relevant; likewise many less formal associations (amateur associations, clubs or special interest groups) have regular newsletters, which could prove a valuable addition to your list.

■ **Commercial magazines:** supermarkets, banks, department stores – many now publish quite sophisticated magazines which are often distributed free to customers. Many accept unsolicited press material from outside their own organization, as it is important that the editorial appears at least semi-independent.

■ **Freelance journalists:** Many journalists, throughout the media, are freelancers often specializing in a certain field. Find out the names of those relevant to your campaign, as they are often looking for good contacts, especially if they can provide material which will help them sell their services.

'Vertical media'

As well as the 'core' media that is of most relevance to your target audiences, also think about 'vertical media' – this term describes those publications or programmes which, although not of central interest to your target, may also be influential. For example, if you are promoting a consultancy service to senior managers in the textile industry, then obviously you'll be targeting textile trade magazines covering industry developments – but don't forget management and business magazines as well. If you are promoting a revolutionary flea collar, then obviously you'll be targeting magazines and programmes for pet lovers – but don't forget 'lifestyle' media as well. By looking at your target groups in this way you'll be able to expand your list, and hopefully increase your media exposure.

Creating a press list

Once you've identified the categories most relevant to your campaign, the next stage is to home in on specific publications and programmes, and start to create a 'media distribution list'. You'll need to create a database comprising the names and addresses of all your target publications or programmes, including the names of correspondents or editors. If your target audiences are very discrete, and the media you wish to target is well known to you, then you may only need to get the latest copy of each publication, or find out the broadcast details of each programme, and compile your list straight away. However, if your list looks like it might be even slightly more extensive, then you should call upon the help of the experts.

A number of well-known organizations exist which provide media listings and distribution services, including access to full details of all media currently published or broadcast at any one time. These lists can be purchased as printed directories or in a variety of electronic formats, and are updated frequently either with new pages (if the directory is ring-bound), new editions or with online updates. Such media databases also provide a wealth of additional information, such as copy deadlines, the type of editorial or photograph preferred and so on, and electronic versions may allow you to add your own information, such as a record of any contact you've had with a relevant journalist, or details of all the information you've dispatched to a particular title.

Media databases can usually be purchased in a variety of ways – usually either as a one-off or as some form of subscription – depending on how important it is that the information you hold is as up to date as possible. Media directories are impressively comprehensive, and provide vast amounts of information on all the categories you can think of. However, they are expensive and you will probably never need to use the majority of the information provided. One advantage of using the services of a PR agency is that they have such databases and directories as part of their stock in trade, and so you can benefit from their investment, and only access the information most relevant to you.

Another option is to use a media services company to handle the entire process of media distribution – writing your release, printing photos, stuffing the envelopes, dispatching material, either electronically (on 'the wire') or by post. Alternatively you can purchase a mailing list as and when required, in the form of printed labels. If you only plan to mail out information once or twice a year, or are planning a one-off mailing to a very extensive audience, then these options can prove to be more cost-effective, saving you the effort of researching and updating your media list.

Creating a press list – even a relatively limited one – can take a lot of time, and so it's important that this time isn't wasted by allowing

the information to get out of date. As with any mailing list, names
and addresses must be checked regularly to ensure they are correct
– and this is particularly important for press material as wrongly
addressed information will often go straight in the bin. The pre-
printed labels, mentioned earlier, are one way of ensuring that
addresses are always up to date, but if you're mailing out press
information on a regular basis then this method can prove very
expensive. The best option is to make sure your list is as precise as
possible, review the national press and broadcast media contacts
quarterly, and go through the rest at least once or twice a year.

Know your press

However limited or extended your media list becomes, a golden
rule is to know what each publication or programme wants before
you start sending them material. If you don't know the nature of the
media you're targeting you won't be able to send information
which they can use, wasting your money, their time and gaining
yourself a bad reputation.

This may seem an unmanageable task, especially if your media list
is as long as your arm, so start by dividing the list into A and B
groups, even C and D if appropriate. The A list will be the most
important and these you really have to get to know inside out. You
probably already receive regular copies of key magazines, or watch
or listen to the most relevant programmes, so you already have a
feel for content, balance and style, and can therefore identify the
type of opportunities which may be available. You'll also quickly
become aware of the approach taken by specific correspondents,
especially those issues in which they take a particular interest.

The other categories on your list need less intensive research – a
media database will be able to tell you some basic facts and figures,
and you may be able to persuade the advertising department of a
magazine to send you a recent back copy in order to give you an
idea of the nature of a particular publication. In reality, however, it
would be impossible for you to read every different regional
newspaper, watch every relevant TV programme or listen to all the
radio programmes which could possibly cover your news. You
should, however, at least attempt to gain a working knowledge of
the different categories of media you want to target, as this will

help you both tailor your information more precisely, and prepare more focused press lists.

A note on electronic media

As with any other computer-based technology, it's impossible to give definitive advice on how to exploit 'new media' opportunities. The speed of change is so fast that new developments arrive on a daily basis, and not least in the field of electronic and online publishing. At time of writing, online magazines – interactive or otherwise – are becoming increasingly popular (at least among publishers and writers), although the response of readers has been less easy to judge. A computer-based medium requires a definite decision from the reader to read – as opposed to the fairly passive activity required of flicking through a printed newsletter – and this necessarily reduces the readership of such online publications. Likewise, the physical difficulties associated with reading on-screen (even though such publications can be printed off) can also serve to dissuade readers.

Online media is certainly at its best when covering news, which can be updated hourly, and the growing number of organizations that circulate news stories online to journalists, or to subscribers of news services, certainly indicates the popularity of the medium for the *dissemination* of news, especially when supported by sophisticated search mechanisms.

We've already touched upon the growth of interactive web-based media, and it's worth reiterating the point that the expansion of specialist programming is worth monitoring, as the opportunities may be exciting in such a content-hungry environment. But as we have already said, audience numbers are not growing so quickly and so you'll have to decide whether it's worth making the effort to get involved.

Virtual press offices

'Latest news' sections are now standard within most web sites and have given rise to the term 'virtual press office', or VPO. As noted above, a web site provides an ideal medium for rapidly changing news, and can also provide easy access to supportive background information. Usually, VPOs comprise copies of press releases, posted on the site as soon as they are released, linked to other relevant pages or even external sites; a searchable press release database allows journalists to scan for more information if they are researching a particular topic in some depth. Email pages directly linked to the press office can also provide a 24-hour contact point, even if the office itself only operates during normal working hours.

If managed efficiently, a VPO can be a valuable asset, and a good site will become popular with journalists in many fields. However, many are simply static repositories for old news. They are not updated as frequently as they should be and this instantly casts doubt on the validity of any information posted – the kiss of death as far as a journalist is concerned. They also still require the positive action of the journalist, and demand time which many simply do not have. If you plan to set up a VPO, then make it as lively and as interactive as the rest of your site, but don't expect it to take any of the burden away from the shoulders of your PR team.

Letting the media know about you – press releases, articles and other ways to send information to the media

You've identified your key target media – now you need to decide how best to let them know about your organization and all the interesting things that it does. This can be done in a number of ways:

- By sending unsolicited material (press releases and so on).
- By contacting journalists directly in order to 'place' editorial, to encourage a journalist to follow a story up in more detail, or simply to try and develop an ongoing relationship.
- By inviting the media to attend or cover a specific event, designed primarily to generate news opportunities – a press launch or other similar occasion.

Although by far the most common item on the PRO's list, the press release is not the only means of gaining coverage in the media, although it is the most commonly used technique. The following options demonstrate the range of opportunities that exist:

Press releases

A press release is the basic building block of a media liaison campaign, and is likely to be the most common type of press information you'll issue. A regular flow of press releases can start to generate consistent coverage in some of your key media; they are also an invaluable foot in the door. If well written and relevant, a press release alerts the journalist to your presence, prompting further contact and certainly giving you an excuse to ring directly to see if you can develop the relationship further.

There is an art to writing a good press release. Your aim is to produce a piece of copy which a journalist can reproduce virtually verbatim, and so the better written the release, the better the chance that it will get used. If a journalist can't grasp the story within the first few lines then the release will be binned, so perfecting the technique of writing press releases is essential – and is one of the reasons why so many PR professionals are ex-journalists. The inclusion of a decent colour photograph also increases the chances of a press release being used, although it may incur some additional costs – this issue is explored later in this section (see page 63).

Despite the growth of electronic media, a hard copy press release, sent by post, is still a very common means of distribution. If timing is not crucial, then hard copy press releases are just as well received as material sent electronically – sometimes better, as often newswires and other services only promote a headline. A physical press release at least gives the journalist the chance to see the full story and glance at any accompanying photos.

What news?

Press releases *only* feature news – so what stories merit a press release? Here are some common examples:

- New products or product developments.
- New services.
- Major contract announcements (mentioning actual sums involved is also good).
- Major business developments (i.e. increased profits, new offices).
- New appointments or promotions.

■ New marketing promotions (i.e. competitions, brochures, web sites).

■ Events (i.e. seminars, conferences, trade shows).

■ Survey results (see page 42).

As you begin to hold regular PR meetings you can literally go down a checklist such as this and identify all the likely material that your organization could supply – and it might be more than you think! It often takes longer than expected to produce press releases, especially if you have to wait for additional information or approval from a third party, so it's often a good idea to have a number in preparation at any one time, then you'll always have something ready for distribution.

Writing a press release

Once you've decided on subject matter then it's time to draft your release. Unfortunately good writing is a talent which is not easy to teach – and you may find that writing succinctly and legibly are hard skills to master at first, and this is why many organizations use professional writers to prepare press information. However, if you take heed of the following guidelines, then your efforts should have a good chance of success:

Layout

■ It's important to adhere to some basic rules of presentation: double type text on one side of the paper only; provide a reference code at the top of the first page, and repeat this code on any subsequent pages, and on any accompanying photographs or transparencies; mark clearly where the press release ends (by typing '——ends——' after the last sentence), and indicate on each sheet how many pages have been used.

■ Always provide a contact name, address, telephone, fax and e-mail address at the end of the main release. Depending on the nature of the news, it's best to give two contacts: the first is usually the person in charge of PR administration, who can provide initial assistance (mark this name 'Press information'), and the second is someone who can answer specific questions on the story involved (mark this name 'Further information').

■ Make sure the words 'Press release' or 'Press information' appear clearly on the first page so that there is no ambiguity about the nature of the information provided. Many organizations have their own press paper specially designed and this is used for all press material. If you only ever intend to issue a limited number of releases then a cheaper alternative is to create a dtp masthead which can be used as a template for all releases.

■ Date the release – usually month and year is sufficient.

■ If necessary, embargo the press release – this means stating the exact date (even time) before which the news should not be used. Embargo dates are usually reserved for stories which are time critical and which are released simultaneously to a number of different media, so that no one is allowed to cover the information exclusively (whether the journalist respects the embargo is another matter!). If you are releasing news ahead of a formal launch event, then an embargo date is also perfectly acceptable – make sure it's clearly indicated right at the front of the release.

Content

■ Any journalist, looking at a press release for the first time, will ask 'so what?' You need to make it crystal clear – from the very first line of copy – *why* the story is news, and *why* it's relevant to that journalist.

■ Title your release clearly and succinctly – it's important to start getting your message across immediately. Don't be tempted to use a jokey or clever-clever headline. As well as hiding the nature of the story, it's the sub-editor's job to write headlines and so it's likely that whatever you produce will be changed anyway. A sub-heading, under the main headline, can help provide further detail if you can't fit all the necessary information succinctly into the title.

■ Never begin the release by writing 'We are pleased to announce ...' or other such portentous phrases. Remember that you are trying to produce a piece of copy that can be used with the minimum of editorial input – how many newspaper articles do you read that begin 'We are pleased ...'?

■ Summarize the whole story in the first paragraph. Journalists will edit a press release from the bottom up and so if they decide that there's only room for a few lines, these will be lifted straight from the opening section – so it's crucial that these few lines get the full story across.

■ Use the second and third paragraphs to expand upon your theme – providing relevant background and additional information to flesh out the basic story. Quotes can lift a press release, as long as they are concise and help the story along. Using a quote from a satisfied customer, for example, can also provide added endorsement. If you are using quotes then make sure they are approved for use first – the issue of approval is examined later in this chapter.

■ Keep both target audiences and target media in mind when writing your release. If you are planning to issue the same news to a variety of media, then you may need to tailor your basic press release to meet the needs of different types of publication or programme – trade or consumer and so on – and different audiences.

■ Opinions may vary, but according to this author, the ideal length for a press release is no more than two pages. However, there may well be additional information that could prove useful to a journalist – company facts and figures for example, or more background to a particular technology. Rather than add these to the body of the release, where they may simply dilute the thrust of the main story, include the information as an 'Editor's note' which is placed at the end of the release, literally after the '——ends——' line.

- ■ If you are hoping to attract the attention of a TV or radio journalist then emphasize any visual aspects of the story, or anything that would be of interest to listeners. You can do this both within the 'body copy' and expand this as an 'Editor's note'.
- ■ If you have included a photograph then add brief details to the bottom of the release, so that the journalist can check that the photo is correct, or can ask for another copy. You could also list other appropriate illustrations which are available and which the journalist could request.

So many instructions! But in practice, these rules provide an almost foolproof way of ensuring that the end result will do its job effectively. So let's see how they work.

Back at Klippits headquarters, the marketing manager is battling with a press release for the gift trade press, which she knows mainly prints short, snappy pieces covering latest products – here's her first attempt:

Klippits now available for gift shops

Klippits is pleased to announce the availability of its new re-usable staple for sale in gift shops. The staple is set to revolutionise offices around the world, as it provides the first, fully re-usable paper fastening system.

Klippits are available in a range of sizes and colours, and are suitable for any type of paper fastening, from two sheets of paper to documents of up to 500 sheets. This system uses a special, flexible metal clip, attached and removed with a special device. Not only does the Klippit hold documents together securely, but it doesn't damage the top and bottom sheets when it is removed.

Klippits will be used in offices and homes – everywhere where anyone needs to keep their papers in order.

For more information, contact Sarah Murray, Marketing Director, Klippits Ltd, Unit 22a, Golding Industrial Estate, Cambridge.

Sarah knows what she wants to say, but is having trouble getting it across. She's also forgotten the needs of her target audience. They need to know not only about the product, but also why they, as gift shop owners, should be selling it.

Let's try and rewrite it for her, remembering the guidelines we established earlier:

PRESS INFORMATION

Ref: KPR1   **August 2001**

Klippits re-usable staple – gift packs now available

The Klippits re-usable paper fastener, launched successfully earlier this year, is now available in a special gift pack, aimed for home office, student and domestic users. The pack comprises a Klippit device, available in a range of unusual designs and colours, and a supply of Klippit fasteners in three sizes. An ideal Christmas gift, the packs will be promoted heavily in the consumer press, and will also be supported by a nationwide advertising campaign.

The gift packs can be supplied loose, or in a specially designed counter-top display, and are available in a range of Christmas and other designs.

The Klippits system uses a flexible metal clip to hold up to 500 pages together safely and securely. The clip is attached and removed with a special device and, unlike other similar systems, top and bottom sheets remain intact when the Klippit is removed.

Launched primarily for the Christmas market, the gift packs will be available all year round.

—ends—

Editor's note

The Klippits system was invented by company founder Michael Lowe as a by-product of his research into re-usable fixing devices for gardeners and nurserymen. Since its launch in 1999, the system has already won a number of awards for its innovative design, including 'Best new stationery product' from the American Association of Stationery Suppliers.

Further information	**Press information**
Sarah Murray	Anna Lowe
Marketing Director	Press Office
Klippits Ltd,	Klippits Ltd
Unit 22a Golding Industrial Estate,	Unit 22a Golding Industrial Estate
Cambridge	Cambridge
Tel: 01223 1234567	Tel: 01223 1234569
Fax: 01223 1234568	Fax: 01223 1234568
e.mail: sm@klippits.co.uk	e.mail: al@klippits.co.uk

Enclosed: Photograph, ref KPR1, caption:
              'The Klippit system is available in a range of Christmas designs'

We've now laid the information out properly, clearly detailed the news, summarized the story in the first paragraph and written the whole piece in a style suited to the target publication – and as I'm sure you'll agree, the end result is already just as you'd expect to read in any trade publication.

Articles

If you look through any trade or consumer publication you'll see a mix of both news stories and longer articles, and many of these articles will have been generated by organizations just like your own, as part of a PR campaign. A longer article obviously brings a range of benefits: more significant exposure in a key publication; a chance to demonstrate knowledge or experience in more detail; a chance to highlight certain individuals and their expertise. Articles can often be ordered as 'off-prints' (full colour reproductions) which can be added to your library of direct mail and other literature.

Most articles are the result of direct research by a journalist, but many are originated by a PRO. Publications often ask organizations directly to produce an article on a specific subject, perhaps following up from a press release; alternatively they can be 'placed' – the PRO contacts an editor to interest them in the story and then writes it for the magazine. A placed article is exclusive to the publication which prints it, cutting down your total exposure within the marketplace but guaranteeing a greater depth of coverage.

Articles can also be sent unsolicited, but these are often shorter and more general pieces, suitable for wider syndication to a number of likely publications, and so exclusivity is less of an issue.

Articles are expected to be less of a 'puff' – not as overtly promotional as a press release, therefore it's important to get the balance right in the text. You are, of course, allowed to mention your organization, but it may simply be as the author of the piece (the 'by-line'), or referred to only once or twice throughout the article.

The presentation of an article is the same as for a press release – double-spaced, clearly referenced and with contact names at the end. The length can vary tremendously – an editor will give you a word count, but if unsolicited you should look to see the average length of other articles similar to your own and tailor it to match. As said above, short articles covering general points should aim to provide no more than half a page of printed copy – so check to see what this represents in the publication you plan to target.

Articles can cover a wide range of subject areas, but broadly speaking they fall into the following categories:

Case histories

An example of how a customer has used your product or service successfully – and a very popular way of showcasing the work of your organization, and demonstrating third-party endorsement. It goes without saying that the more familiar the customer name, the greater the impact of the story, but such stories do have to be handled with care. Your customer must be completely happy about the use of their name within an article which is essentially promoting your organization, and many are wary of giving away information which they may feel to be of benefit to their competitors. But such stories also give your customers free PR, so as a rule they are usually delighted to help.

Case histories follow a fairly straightforward pattern: what was the problem?; what was the solution?; why was your organization involved?; what benefits did you offer?; why was the end result a success? The aim of the story is to profile the work of your organization, and the more interesting the context the more attractive the story will be to the journalist. A range of good illustrations to support the editorial is essential.

Case histories can take time to produce, but even so extend your schedule when dealing with third parties – gaining agreement to go ahead, conducting the interviews, and then finally gaining their written approval to use the material (see page 67 for more on this) can all take longer than expected, especially as you are asking a favour of your client or customer – you can't really chivvy them along if they are dragging their heels. The best you can do is to make them well aware of any deadlines before they agree to contribute.

Discursive articles

If you or your organization takes a particular stand on a particular issue then your opinions may prove ideal subject matter for an article, especially if the issue in question is topical or controversial. Discursive articles are often used as a way of promoting a specific person – say a managing director – and as a way of demonstrating the ethos of an organization. Such articles work best if they raise controversial issues, and so you must be sure you can cope with any criticism which may result. Often a head shot of the author of the piece is all that is required by way of illustration – but make sure it is a professional portrait, not a shot from a 'photo-me' booth!

Informative articles

An article which focuses closely upon a specific area of expertise – an aspect of technology for example, a legal issue, or the close examination of a legislative change – can also demonstrate the credentials of an individual, and by default, the knowledge and experience of an organization as a whole. Once again, topical issues are often the best source of subject matter, and many editors are glad to be offered ready-made copy on a subject about which they may know very little. Diagrams, figures and other supporting illustrations will all be welcomed.

Article synopses

Rather than spend time writing a fully fleshed out article (which can take longer than one thinks) a good idea is to send a synopsis of the article to an editor, to gauge their opinion. If they want to go ahead, then you can write the article, tailoring it closely to the style of the publication. If not, then you have not wasted any time, and can always send the synopsis on to another magazine.

Forthcoming feature diary

Most trade publications publish schedules of 'special features' planned for the year ahead, and issue them as part of their 'media pack'. Although these planned features are designed primarily as a focus for advertising, relevant editorial contributions may also be welcomed. By maintaining a diary of these forthcoming features, material can be prepared well in advance in order to ensure editorial coverage in the most relevant issue of the magazine's year. It's a good idea to call the features editor ahead of the copy deadline to see exactly what type of material the feature will cover. Often such conversations prompt requests for longer articles, or for material that can be used in later editions of the magazine. Existing press releases, articles and photographs can be built up into a library of approved information that can be dispatched quickly when such opportunities arise.

Surveys

Many organizations commission surveys primarily to generate news for press releases – many of these become annual events, and are therefore covered in even more depth as past results can be compared. Surveys can range enormously in both subject matter and scope – but all will be underpinned by the core aims of your PR strategy. For example, if your main aim is to promote a brand of pet food, then a survey into the most popular names for dogs could provide some interesting, newsworthy results, and gain a lot of coverage in the consumer press which will be among your key target media. If you are promoting a service aimed at accountants, then a survey into a particular business trend would produce material for more serious releases. If a specially commissioned survey is too time consuming and too expensive to consider, then a cheaper option is to tag some appropriate questions on to any other market research or customer feedback mechanisms that you already have in place.

Syndicated tapes and video news releases

Prepared for distribution to independent radio and TV stations, taped interviews on topics of general interest are often used as an infill on daytime schedules. These are primarily a tool of the consumer PR campaign, although they are also used within feature programmes. The use of pre-recorded coverage as instant backup for a breaking news story is also a well-tried route. Video news releases perform the same job but obviously use video, and combine stock footage of buildings, people etc. with footage directly relevant to the news story – interviews for example, or shots of a product being launched.

Both video and audio tapes can be expensive to produce, and their success will be limited if they are not professionally edited and distributed. If you think that this technique could be useful in your campaign, then it's best to contact one of the many companies specialising in this service, who can handle the entire process – from script writing to monitoring coverage.

Syndicated columns

As well as producing in-depth articles, written in response to a specific topic or issue, another idea is to create a 'column' which could be issued regularly. These are often picked up by copy-hungry regional press, especially in regular features such as business pages, but less so by other categories of press, although you could consider negotiating the production of such a column specifically for a key publication if you know that it already carries features of a similar type.

Content could be topical ('what to do in the garden this month') or problem based, providing an answer to a typical scenario. Although often used within consumer campaigns, regular advice columns are very popular in business sections – usually the newspaper in question feels honour bound to offer the same opportunity to a number of similar local organizations (lawyers, for example, or accountants) in order to avoid accusations of favouritism, but even so, your name should be one of those regularly occurring if such an opportunity is available.

If you plan a widespread syndication, try to select publications which do not overlap, either in subject matter or the geographical spread of their readership, to allay an editor's fears of repetition and to give limited exclusivity. Include a brief covering letter with the first column you issue, asking whether the editor would like to receive further columns on a regular basis – the responses will help you establish a regular mailing list. Given the pressures on a journalist's time, you can also telechase the form if you want to ensure distribution, offering the column to another publication wherever a first choice refuses.

Media Guide

Many journalists cover an increasingly diverse range of stories, but as they know they cannot be an expert in eveything they rely on their specialist contacts to supply them with relevant information as and when required. A 'Media Guide' is a useful means of supplying journalists with a list of such contacts, in the hope that – if a particular issue comes to the fore – you or your organization will be contacted to provide expert comment. Such a Guide needs not be extensive – although those produced by major organizations can be the size of a small book. First identify the topics on which you would like to be well known, then put names to these topics – it doesn't matter if the same name appears more than once. Update the list regularly, as your knowledge expands, or as new members join your team. Make sure that the individuals you've listed are happy talking to the press – if not then you may have to consider finding an alternative, or arrange for some media training (see page 53 for more information).

Comment

If your organization is closely involved in, is related to, or has a strong opinion on an issue that is currently in the news, then you may often feel that you could add to much of the 'expert comment' used on news programmes and in the press. If so, then scan the national press daily so that relevant stories can be flagged as they break, and the journalists who cover them identified. Rather than waiting to be asked, you can then provide comment on the story either by either e.mailing or faxing a brief statement through to the relevant journalist or newsdesk – often journalists will be looking for quotes to include as quickly as possible, and if one arrives ready made then they may pick it up and use it. But whatever you do, make sure your response reaches the journal in time for the next edition.

A less immediate response is to draft a letter to the editor, putting your comments into a broader context. The wide circulation of the Media Guide will also help encourage direct requests.

Advertorials

More and more, publications of every type exploit the desire of organizations to see their names in print by offering advertorials. These are full articles presented in the style of the publication, and although they are designed to blend in seamlessly with the surrounding copy, they will have the phrase 'advertisement feature', or something similar, printed on the page. Advertorials can range in extent from a modest half page to a full front-cover wraparound, hiding the real front cover beneath. They are usually paid for by the organization featured, the cost reflecting the nature and prominence of the piece. Some advertorials (especially those in the local press) can be funded by the advertisements which surround the main article ('Bob Jones the Butcher is pleased to support ...' and so on.).

If written properly and planned well, then an advertorial can be a good method of gaining exposure in a target publication, especially if the timing of such exposure is important – a shop opening for example, an appearance at an exhibition, the arrival of a roadshow or a product launch. It can also build a close link with the target audience, by appearing to support a favoured publication. Advertorials can also be used to effectively promote a number of different messages at once (if you're launching a product range for example) or to explain a complex message in more detail – if you need to deliver important information which must be reproduced in full.

The greatest advantage of the advertorial is the control it offers over content – although the publication will demand to see and approve the text that is going to be used. It does pay to have the copy written by a professional copywriter – not only will it read more effectively, but a skilful writer will be able to produce an article which blends in with the style of the surrounding pages. Most publications offering advertorials will also offer the services of a journalist who can write the article for you, for a fee.

Although less 'in-your-face' than pure advertising, the advertorial's greatest disadvantage, of course, is that the reader will soon realize that the article is not bona fide editorial, and react accordingly.

Competitions and giveaways

Most of the giveaways (free samples for the first xx readers to respond) and competitions you see featured in the media have been placed by PROs although, just as with advertorials, many magazines increasingly offer structured opportunities for free gifts and other such promotions. Obviously, these activities are well suited to product PR as the product itself can provide the prize, but service organizations can also employ similar strategies, offering their services for free, or simply stumping up cash and using the competition for pure promotion.

Competitions and special offers vary in scope enormously – from word searches to national Award programmes, with prizes ranging from money-off coupons to round the world holidays. Some competitions result in sustained coverage over a period of weeks, others appear just on one day. Whatever you decide to do, make sure that you can handle any administration necessary, and establish clearly where responsibilities lie for jobs such as selecting winners and dispatching prizes.

If a competition would suit your target audiences, and would fit in with the aims of your overall campaign, then a good way to decide what to do is to look at what the main types of media demand:

■ **Regional media** love free gifts, giveaways and competitions, and you can syndicate these in the same way as a column (above) – but this time demand a positive response from the editor before going ahead. A quick review of your own local media will indicate the level at which most competitions are pitched (most are no more than a lucky draw) and prize value can be quite low.

■ **Trade press:** once again, glance through your key publications to see what is currently being featured. Competitions are common, if the prize is of a reasonable value and relevant to the readership, and these are often run in conjunction with the title. The trade press is more open to the concept of the 'Award', in order to show specific recognition of achievement within an industry (see below).

■ **National daily and consumer media:** competitions are commonplace in the national media, and are often used to actively sell publications or to attract readers or listeners, so exposure will be high but prize value is usually high – contact the paper or magazine you have in mind to establish their minimum prize value before you even begin to consider this as an option. Giveaway slots have become increasingly popular – once again a minimum number of items, or a minimum total product value may be demanded from you and you will have to make sure that you can supply the numbers promised.

Award schemes

Although perhaps not strictly speaking purely a media liaison activity (more often coming under the banner of sponsorship), Awards schemes are often promoted jointly with relevant media. The benefits are clear – guaranteed exposure and publicity for a sustained period, direct association with a key media vehicle and direct association with a campaign to promote or reward achievement in a specific field. Many Awards are set up with the declared intent of becoming an annual event, thus sustaining the sponsors' involvement over an even longer timespan.

Awards can be given to almost anything or anyone, and can be employed within any type of PR programme. Although Award schemes can be sustained for many months, resulting in considerable exposure, prize value may have to be quite high in order to encourage a high number of entrants of sufficient quality. There is also the added complication of entry administration and judging, and often an event such as a dinner will be required to round off the whole activity, increasing your final budget.

Using celebrities

A celebrity can be used to attract even more attention to a news story, usually an event such as an opening ceremony, a party, or even speaking at a conference. A celebrity can provide unspoken endorsement of your organization, and will also relate very directly to a particular audience type – and so for these reasons if you decide to use a celebrity make sure you choose the right person very carefully.

Celebrities do not come cheap, and the better-known they are the more they charge. Even if you can afford them, there's no guarantee that your first choice will be available, if they don't like the event you have in mind, or if their diaries are already booked. Celebrity booking agencies exist which can help you if you decide to follow this route, as can the agents of the individual celebrities themselves.

Contacting journalists directly

Rather than sending unsolicited material to a journalist, another option is to make direct contact. This may seem like the fastest route to media attention, but even the most seasoned PR professionals only use this technique when they have something concrete to offer – something that they know should be of real interest.

Many PROs bother journalists with irrelevant information, or bother them too often or at the wrong time; as a result, many journalists have developed a love/hate relationship with the PR industry, and can often be quite abrasive when contacted. Simply remember that many journalists cannot survive without input, in some form or other, from PROs and that if you have something valid to offer then the journalist should listen.

When to call? In the vast majority of cases, the press material you generate will not merit direct contact, but in the following situations a phone call could be the best course of action:

You want to offer an exclusive

For example, if you have a case study which would be ideal for one of your key target publications, then ring the features editor or relevant correspondent and try to 'place' the article as an exclusive – gaining their agreement to publish the story in a specific issue, and in return guaranteeing that the material will only appear in that publication. The journalist may then decide to write up the story themselves, but it's far more likely that you will have to produce the article by a given deadline, which will at least give you control over content and message.

You want to comment on a current issue

If time is of the essence, then direct contact is the best way to contribute to a story currently in the headlines. If you have a relevant case history for example, or can provide expert comment, then go directly to the journalist covering the story (in whatever media is most appropriate to your campaign) and offer to help in any way you can. Journalists remember contacts who have given them useful material and will return to the same source whenever appropriate.

You want to develop a relationship with key journalists

The more you issue regular press releases to the core media on your press list, and the more coverage you generate, then the more you'll start to think about 'making contacts'. Although productive relationships can be developed in this way, the value of 'contacts' is often oversold by the PR industry. Journalism is a very mobile profession, and individuals move from title to title, or programme to programme with remarkable speed. If the quality of your story is good enough, then a journalist will use it whether they've known you for years, or are new in the job. However, as we noted above, from the journalist's point of view, a good contact is worth it's weight in gold so if you know you can supply relevant, reliable information on a regular basis, then trying to forge a more direct relationship is certainly worth attempting.

Once again, you need to find a purpose for making the call – journalists rarely have time to chew the fat – so use excuses such as recent coverage of your news (offer to provide an article expanding on the press release that was used), or call to discuss a forthcoming feature to find out more about editorial opportunities. If relevant to your media campaign, national stringers and freelancers (see page 28) are certainly worth getting to know. They are always on the lookout for interesting stories and often work on behalf of more than one publication or programme. If your local community is an important target audience, then try and get to know local journalists – many are well-known figures in their own right, and can be valuable allies in time of crisis.

Whatever you choose to do, however, make sure you angle your story for the readership rather than for the perceived personality of the journalist, as you are then more likely to hit the right note.

If you plan to use direct contact within your media campaign then it's important to understand the way in which a journalist works, if your efforts are to be successful. The following guidelines should prove useful:

- Monthly and weekly magazines have set copy dead-lines and this information can be obtained directly from the publication itself. Make sure any contact you make is well before a deadline if your aim is to appear in the next edition. Certainly avoid the period immediately before publication, when the next issue is being 'put to bed', as the journalist will be too busy to pay attention to your call.

- The best time to contact a journalist working on a national daily newspaper is between 11 and 12 in the morning. Editorial meetings will be over and there will still be plenty of time to follow up any interesting leads before the next deadline. Between 2 and 3 in the afternoon is another window of opportunity.

- For journalists working on Sunday papers, Tuesdays or Wednesdays are the best days to get in touch.

■ If your target is a journalist working in the broadcast media then it depends upon the nature of their current assignment as to when to make contact: news reporters may be working to hourly deadlines; feature reporters may be working on a series of programmes at a time, and so will be less constrained. The best approach is to make an initial call to find out, if nothing else, the best time to call back!

■ Many – although not all – journalists can be abrupt or even rude when answering unsolicited calls (usually those working in national or larger regional media). As emphasized above, don't call unless you have something relevant to say and have additional material ready to fax or e-mail. Make sure you can answer the most obvious questions – or if you can't, then have someone to hand who can. Get to the point as quickly as possible, allowing the journalist to decide immediately whether or not to continue the conversation.

■ Never ring to ask why a press release wasn't used – it will do your relationship with the media no good at all! Instead review the release at your next evaluation meeting, and try to work out why it wasn't printed (see Chapter 11 for more).

■ Visiting key journalists in person can prove a worthwhile exercise. If you are targeting trade press, then you'll soon find that many publications share the same building so you can easily visit a number of journalists in one day. Make firm appointments in advance, rather than turn up unannounced, and don't go empty handed. Take along a few ideas for stories, making sure you have at least one possible exclusive for each publication you visit, and also take along a good range of background information. Look at your Forthcoming Feature Diary for even more ideas. You may end up only spending a few minutes chatting in the reception area, but you will have strengthened a potentially valuable contact, and allowed the journalist to put a face to a name.

■ Always keep a record of any contact you have had with a journalist: who called; when they called; what they wanted; how you responded. You'll soon build up a database of contacts who have shown positive interest in your organization, and details of the type of story in which they are interested.

If a journalist calls you

If your media campaign is starting to generate positive interest, then you should find that journalists start to call you – especially if you become well known as a source of expertise (see Media Guide, page 44), or as a 'good example' of a particular industry or trend. On the other hand, if you have attracted bad publicity, then journalists may hound you for less positive reasons.

Whatever the circumstances, don't panic if a journalist calls – remember the following golden rules:

■ Don't feel obliged to provide off-the-cuff answers if a journalist demands an instant response (usually because they have a pressing deadline). Simply determine the nature of the questions they want to ask and say you'll call back in five minutes with your answers. This allows you to get your thoughts in order, and to consult colleagues if you need additional information. However, don't leave an under-prepared PRO to handle the call for you if you don't want to talk to a journalist. Either brief your PRO properly or hand the call to a colleague who is equally well informed.

■ Never say 'no comment' – it implies that you are either hiding facts or are running scared from a situation. Instead, issue a simple holding statement, giving reasons why only limited information is available, and indicating when a fuller statement will be available. This is a much more positive response, and maintains your good reputation. If the issue is controversial then work out your response well in advance (see Chapter 8 for more on this).

- ■ 'Off the record' is another remark to be avoided, unless you know and trust the journalist in question, or can be sure that the information won't cause serious damage if 'inadvertently' used.

- ■ If you promise to return a journalist's call then do so as quickly as possible. You don't know when their deadline is, and if they can't get a comment from you, then they'll simply call the next contact on their list – probably a rival organization. Make sure procedures are in place to handle journalist calls when you're not available, so that vital opportunities aren't wasted.

- ■ Devise a 'Journalist contact form' and give a supply to anyone who may speak to the media. Such a form will simply record the name of the journalist, the publication or programme they represented, what they wanted to know and what was the response. The results will form the basis of your 'good contacts' database and also prove very useful in evaluation.

If the prospect of talking to a journalist worries you, but you know that it will become an important part of your job, then consider a Media Training course. Often run by current or former journalists, these courses allow you to develop and practise the skills needed to deal with print and broadcast media in a variety of situations, and can prove invaluable in building confidence.

Press conferences and launches

Inviting the press to witness the unveiling of a new product or to hear the formal announcement of interesting news can prove highly effective: it can focus attention clearly on your news, hopefully gaining consistent, simultaneous coverage across a broad range of different media; it can provide an opportunity for you to contact and hopefully meet many of the journalists with whom you'd like to do more in future; and it can provide a good excuse for corporate entertainment – getting satisfied customers together in the same room is always good for business, and if they have a chance to talk to a journalist then even better!

However, press launches can be expensive and time consuming to organize and can produce relatively disappointing results. Journalists' diaries fill up rapidly with very similar invitations, and the decision to attend may only be made a day or two beforehand – as a result, pre-launch planning can be very frustrating as numbers continually fluctuate, and your launch is constantly in competition with other events, and other news, which may be breaking on the same day. If your media list mainly comprises trade press, then it's also worth remembering that not all trade publications are city-based, so finding a venue convenient for all may be difficult.

All in all, it's best to view press launches more as an opportunity for corporate hospitality, networking and as a staff 'thank you' than as an exclusive media event – if you broaden the scope of the event in this way, then you've more chance of being successful in at least one of your aims.

Planning a press conference

Press conferences need meticulous organization: the following checklist will provide a good starting point, but if you are planning to hold such an event it may be worth hiring the services of a PR professional to make sure the end result is as successful as possible, and provide much needed support for your own staff who could easily be overwhelmed by the amount of planning and administration necessary. Consider:

Venue

An interesting venue, relevant to the occasion, can certainly encourage attendance. Many unusual buildings, museums or other public spaces are now available for hire and so it's worth doing some creative thinking and looking around, rather than hiring a faceless room in a boring hotel. However, whatever the nature of the venue, make sure the nature of the space available suits your needs – for example, it's often a good idea to choose a room which can be divided up into a reception area and a 'theatre' area, enabling guests to leave their dirty cups and saucers behind when the presentation begins. Make sure the space will suit the potential size of your audience, that the room is large enough to handle all the expected guests, but not too large to make them feel uncomfortable.

Also check that the venue has the following:

- easy access (or parking);
- if necessary, enough space to allow film crews (or your own video team) to set up their equipment;
- smaller rooms for private interviews (between press and speakers);
- good availability, preferably from the evening before, so that any stands and displays can be set up well in advance;
- AV, phone, fax and computer links as necessary;
- catering facilities, or permission to serve food and drink.

Timing

It may seem obvious, but try to pick a time when you can hope to gain as much attention as possible. Don't pick a date when journalists may all be attending a major trade fair in an associated industry; don't pick a day when there is a national 'event' happening – directories of such events, days and even weeks (usually associated with some other PR campaign) are available for further information. You can't control every eventuality, of course, and if a major story breaks on the morning of your event, sending all your invited journalists running in the opposite direction then you will just have to put it down to bad luck.

If you want to achieve coverage in the national press, time the conference for the morning and dispatch a press release covering the event to a news agency by noon – the agency will then electronically distribute the release to your press list, along with any photographs. Guests can stay on for as long as they like over lunch, but do not expect many journalists to do so – some will even leave before the presentation finishes, so make sure all press packs are available on arrival, and that interviews can be set up before the event starts. Picking a day early in the week will also enable Sunday journalists to use the story.

Press invitations

Inviting the press to a launch event requires more than just an invitation – you really need to work hard to persuade a journalist that it's worth the time spent away from a crowded desk. So what should your invitation pack comprise? Here's the belt and braces approach – prepare:

- **a basic, embargoed press release**, providing essential information. If the event itself is part of the news – it's an Award ceremony for example, or an important announcement will be made by an important person – then include those details in the release. Otherwise, simply focus on the story – the event is just another mechanism for getting the message across to the media. Include a photograph if possible.

- **a letter** explaining why the journalists should attend, listing points which can't be made in the release: the relevance of the news opportunities, other interesting guests who could be interviewed, or the range of other products or technologies on display – even the venue if you think it might be a draw. Lay out the text using bullet points, emboldened script and so on, so that a journalist can pick up on key points straight away.

- **an event timetable** listing start times; slots allotted to photography (these should take place just before and after the main event); the presentation itself, plus the timing of individual speakers or demonstrations; Q&A and interview opportunities; and when lunch or other refreshments are going to be served.

- **directions** to the venue.

- **a detailed response form**, (for fax or email return) allowing the journalist to indicate if they will attend, and if they require any special arrangements i.e. for filming, recording radio interviews, photography or for interviews with speakers.

In order to catch the eye of jaded journalists, invitations can take on increasingly bizarre or complex formats, but most journalists will base their acceptance on the quality of the story. However, there is no harm in trying to design an eye-catching invitation card or including a small gift relevant to the event – and it is often said that gold edged invitations prompt a better response that those with no edging at all!

Press invitations should be issued at least four weeks in advance of the event itself, but don't be surprised if only a handful of reply forms are returned. As already mentioned, most newsdesks or editorial managers look at their diaries week by week, to assess all opportunities. Following up invitations by phone is worthwhile and should start two weeks before the event. Although arduous and time consuming it can increase attendance dramatically, as many journalists will have lost or forgotten the information, or may have never even received it. You can entrust this 'phone around' to junior members of your marketing team, but make sure you have senior staff on hand to answer any detailed questions.

The presentation

Follow the same advice given to anyone preparing for and delivering a presentation – and there are plenty of books on the subject which offer endless information and useful tips. Structure the content of your presentation along the same lines as a press release – start by summarizing the main story, underlining the most important points, and then go into further detail as necessary. If a detailed technical explanation is required, then it may be useful to share the stage with an expert in this particular field as they will be particularly useful during the question and answer sessions.

The whole presentation should last no more than 45 minutes, and time for questions should be ample. You may find, however, that many journalists may want to interview the speaker in private immediately after the event, so make sure this can be handled easily.

Displays and presentations

Use the event as an excuse to promote your organization as much as possible. Make the venue as attractive as possible, with relevant displays, and ample supplies of marketing material, particularly in the reception area, where guests can view it at their leisure.

Press packs

Information packs should be created for press, and should contain further information on the subject being presented, and general background information on your organization. Press packs should also contain a press release on the event, relevant photographs, and potted biographies of the speakers – don't worry about being too comprehensive, as most journalists will expect to receive the most relevant information ahead of the event, and to gain the extra detail they need from the event itself.

Although officially available only on departure, many press will want to receive the information straight away, especially if they have to leave the event before it officially finishes, so make sure press packs are available on arrival.

During the event

A welcome desk should be staffed throughout the event, and should ideally be placed outside the main room, so that late journalists can be welcomed without disturbing proceedings. Name badges must be handed out to guests as they arrive. These can be colour-coded to indicate members of the press, your staff and any other guests you have added to the list. No member of the press should be left alone during the event. They will be expecting to meet as many people as possible in order to make the time spent worthwhile, so brief staff to make sure that someone is always in attendance.

Post-event

Invited journalists who fail to turn up must be sent a press pack as soon as possible, and any specific press queries which couldn't be handled at the event should be dealt with ideally the same day, or as soon as you get back to your desk.

'Bad press' – what to do

There may be no such thing as bad publicity, but if you ever experience negative coverage then your reaction may be less sanguine. The risk of bad press goes hand in hand with a proactive media campaign. Many larger organizations, especially those with a well-established public image, garner bad publicity on a regular basis, and although they don't treat it lightly neither do they seek to challenge every instance of misrepresentation. Likewise, if you suddenly receive worrying coverage, then your first reaction should not be to panic or to harangue the journalist responsible, but to carefully assess the situation and take appropriate action – and we'll look at some examples of responses below.

Time is of the essence

Whatever happens, it is important that you act quickly. Time really is of the essence, especially given the ephemeral nature of most media and the short memory of readers, viewers or listeners. Of course, this short memory can work to your advantage, but if you actively want to correct a wrong then you need to do it as quickly as you can, whilst the original piece is still reasonably fresh. It's also important that senior staff take on as much of the firefighting as possible, hand in hand with the PRO. If specific points are being countered, or arguments developed, then the journalist will want to talk to someone with all the relevant information to hand – not to a PRO who needs to refer to someone else when responding to key questions. Use your PRO to draft responses and guide actions – not to take the flack.

As we mentioned above, the greater your public profile the higher the risk of bad publicity, but no organization should consider itself immune. Here are some of the more common scenarios, and advice on how to react:

Wrong information

If a newspaper prints the wrong dates for a seminar for example, or a trade magazine misprints a crucial detail within a technical specification, then you'll certainly have the right to groan inwardly and take action. Go through the following steps as quickly as you can:

- Check your original press release or article – make sure the mistake is not your fault, or the fault of any third party which helped you prepare the information.
- If your press information was correct, contact the offending publication or programme immediately and point out the mistake. Ask if a correction can be

printed or broadcast as soon and as prominently as possible – ideally on the same page or at the same point in the programme as the erroneous information occurred. Most editors are happy to correct genuine errors, but they cannot give you a guarantee, especially if more important news breaks in the interim and available space is suddenly at a premium.

■ Judge the overall impact of the error and act accordingly. If it appeared in a relatively unimportant publication, then requesting a correction is probably sufficient. If it occurred in one of your key media, in the piece which you hoped was going to gain you most publicity then you may need to do more. Use your web site to provide an additional response – overtly flagging up the mistake if necessary. Brief any staff members who may start to receive queries from your customers or other contacts: give them full details of the error, and an approved response.

■ If the error came from you, then more urgent action will be needed, depending on the predicted level of impact. To take the example of the seminar again: if you've mailed the wrong date to a press list of 50 publications, then you need to e.mail or fax them immediately with the correct information. Prioritize those contacts with the most pressing deadlines – if you're lucky, they may not yet have used the wrong information, and you can also phone to confirm that the correction has got through and has a chance of being used. Those media with weekly or monthly deadlines are less urgent, but nevertheless, if the incorrect detail is potentially damaging, then phone to ensure that the correction has been received.

■ Mistakes do happen even in the best regulated press office, but if you ever experience a scare such as this then you certainly won't want it to happen again. Undergo a post-mortem after the event to identify what went wrong. If you have kept your signed and approved drafts, background information and notes, then you'll quickly be able to identify where the mistake originated, and how it slipped through the net. Did senior staff delegate approval to junior PROs due to pressures of time? Do you need extra approval loops to prevent this from happening again? The effort needed to rectify even the smallest mistake will help convince management that PR shouldn't always be an afterthought or the responsibility of juniors.

■ If the mistake came from a third party – wrong information from a co-sponsor for example, or a client in a case study – then you need to let them know what has happened as soon as possible, and ideally agree to share the burden of administering the correction procedure. Once again, a review of your approvals process may be needed. Did your external contact fully appreciate the importance of thoroughly checking the information? Did you accept the word of a junior staff member when you should have held out for more senior approval?

Critical coverage

You cannot always guarantee verbatim coverage of your news, and the more you edge into the limelight the greater the chance of critical coverage at some point. This is particularly true if you are supporting or promoting a more controversial argument or cause.

If such negative coverage appears, then the following actions should be considered:

■ Evaluate the impact of the coverage (see page 167, Chapter 11, for more on how to quantify impact). Can you afford to simply let it go or do you want or need to respond?

■ If you decide that you are justified to demand a right of reply, then analyse the coverage in detail, and prepare a response based on each point raised, with additional arguments if necessary. When you have your counter-argument clear in your head, contact the author of the piece (assuming it's a staff writer) or the editor of the publication or programme and outline your reaction and the response you want to give. **Don't** phone the journalist before you have put your thoughts in order. You run the risk of being angry and your argument becoming incoherent, and you certainly don't want to alienate either the journalist or the programme or publication – both could be valuable allies in the future. If you're lucky, you may be invited to submit a response for publication or broadcast – but even if this option is denied, you will at least have opened up a dialogue with an interested journalist which may prove useful later in your campaign.

■ If tackling the author of the piece seems over the top, then consider responding via the letters page or to a feedback programme, if one exists. If the criticism extends to other members of your industry then you could encourage organizations similar to your own to write in and give their views – your trade association or local business allies could also help.

■ Once again, after the event, undertake a post-mortem. Why was the coverage negative? Was the criticism justified? If it was, what are you doing about it and can any positive PR be undertaken in response? If the criticism seems unfair, why was it made in the first place? Once again, can any PR be implemented to help promote a more positive view?

Misleading coverage

If you are the subject of actively misleading press then you may have greater cause for concern, and could even consider taking legal advice if you think that the coverage will have damaging repercussions. If the coverage is less worrying, then follow the steps outlined above: prepare your counter-argument; contact the journalist or editor; try to get your side of the story covered one way or another. Being able to prove that the coverage was misleading gives you more leverage when it comes to gaining a right of reply, so exploit this advantage as much as possible. You may also wish to publish your response on your website, and have it to hand should any client or other contact get in touch.

Damning coverage

If you suddenly become the focus of concentrated, negative media attention, then you need to react more comprehensively. Once again, analysis of legal considerations, relative impact, and the lifetime of the coverage all needs to be made, but if poor press starts to snowball then it can change the climate of opinion about your organization very quickly. If you suspect – or can foresee – that this is starting to happen, then key elements of the crisis management plan need to be put in place. See Chapter 8 for more on this.

Photographs and other illustrations

Photographs play an important role in a media campaign, and you will have noticed that they should be included wherever appropriate – with press releases, with articles and so on. In many cases a good photo will increase the chance of information being used, as the editor will want to use good photography wherever possible – you may even be able to suggest a front cover placement if the shot is particularly good. You'll probably already have a library of relevant shots – products, people, buildings and so on – generated for other marketing activities: many of these will be fine for PR activities, but you must pass a critical eye over them before they are used, as the demands of a magazine are different to those of your company brochure. Photographs for media work tend to be clear, straightforward, and demonstrate (if possible) the main messages of the press release. Brochure photography can tend towards the more conceptual, and is often designed to be used within the context of a layout or with other shots, making it less appropriate for press applications.

New photographs are usually commissioned for use with press releases, adding to the newsworthiness of the whole item. Use a photographer experienced in press work – you'll find that many also work for local newspapers, and so will know what is needed. Glancing through any of your target media will soon indicate the type of photograph which works well in a specific context, and your photographer will also be able to advise you on how to set up or stage the shot so that it gives the same message as your press release. Try not to produce photographs which are *too* conventional. And if you need to use a photograph of people – appointments, contracts, visitors or whatever – then try to avoid the usual shots of people shaking hands, or grouped around the desk pointing awkwardly at a piece of paper (or even worse, holding the phone). These really are hackneyed images, and will actively dissuade people from reading further. Instead try to place people against unusual backdrops or in less formal poses.

Illustrations such as drawings, diagrams or logos can also be used, but usually to accompany articles or longer pieces. If these are already stored electronically then they can be offered as files for direct import into the publication's system – if not then produce as good a top copy as possible, and cross-reference it to the article as you would with a photograph.

Captions

Provide a caption for every photograph or illustration you supply – not just for information, but also as instant copy that can be used as a caption on the page. You should of course explain what's in the picture, but you should also tie the caption into the promotional aims of the accompanying article or press release. For example, if you are sending a photo of your latest model of desk lamp, don't just say 'The latest model of desk lamp from Brite Ideas Ltd' – instead, caption it 'The latest desk lamp from Brite Ideas represents stylish design at a bargain price'.

Photographs of people should be captioned in a more straightforward way, clearly indicating name and job title, and who is who if there is more than one person.

Format

Use colour for all photographs. As even the national papers now use colour on a regular basis, it's a safer option than producing a black and white image which cannot be converted – colour can at least always be reproduced in black and white! A standard 5″ × 8″ shot will be perfectly adequate for press releases – if you are putting together a bundle of material to accompany an article then you need not be so strict, although you may want to double check to make sure that your target publication is happy to accept photos of the type you have available.

Your photographer will supply referenced prints – keep a note of this reference in your photo library (see above) to enable quick reordering if necessary.

Copyright

Legally, the copyright of photographs resides with the photographer which is the reason why they keep hold of the negatives; this does not necessarily restrict your use of the images you've commissioned, but it does prevent you from reproducing the original photograph without the photographer's consent. Don't worry unduly about this – simply ask your photographer to explain the implications of copyright with regard to your own PR campaign.

Colour separation charges

Many publications now levy a fee for the reproduction of photographs – a colour separation charge – and annoying though these can be, they are unavoidable. They are a source of extra revenue for the title in question, and are prevalent across all publications, from the prestigious to the humble. There is little you can do to avoid paying them, other than say no and run the risk (unfortunately quite high) that your press release will not be featured. Many organizations see them as a necessary evil and attach a budget to each release in order to cover this cost. If the photo is good enough, then you may find it gets used anyway, but you can't guarantee this will happen.

Running a media campaign – administration

A successful media campaign depends greatly upon good administration – and the broader the scope and range of your programme of activities, the greater the administrative support you'll need. So it's important that you have resources in place right from the start. Senior management input is essential, to make sure everything continues to run as smoothly and as effectively as possible. Administration is usually left to a junior member of the marketing team: although often tedious, and repetitive, it provides an excellent insight into what a PR campaign actually comprises, and provides the basic raw material for your final evaluation.

Media campaign administration focuses on the following:

Managing press lists and contact databases

The extent of this job depends greatly upon the nature of the campaign you are planning to run. As we mentioned earlier, you may decide that buying contact details as and when you want them, or hiring an agency to manage despatch is in fact the best way to control your list. If you decide to create a press list on your own, then keeping the information up to date is very important. Whoever is in charge of managing the press list must check it at least once a quarter – although addresses will remain reasonably static, journalists will change.

Managing distribution

As we've already discussed, although electronic dispatch is growing increasingly common, the straightforward mailing of hard copy press releases is still a valid means of distributing information – especially to the smaller, more specialized trade press, and certainly if the story is not highly topical. As a result, there is always going to be a job stuffing envelopes and sticking stamps, which is usually as easy to manage in-house unless your press list is huge, and then – again – there are plenty of agencies who can help you.

Records need to be kept of what was sent to which publication, when, if any photos were also included, and ideally what results were achieved.

Providing a first point of contact

You may want to actively name your administration assistant on any press releases or articles as the contact for 'press information' (if they are capable of handling enquiries efficiently). Even though a journalist will want to talk to an expert, it's useful to have someone readily available to manage the initial conversation, liaise with senior colleagues and deal with any immediate requests – for photos or background information for example.

Approval systems

Approval systems need to be put in place and followed to the letter, to make sure that nothing is dispatched to the press accidentally. Signatures must be gained from all relevant personnel before any material can be issued, to make sure it has been read and approved, and these signed copies must be stored carefully.

If you want to mention the name of any third party in any media information, then you need to gain approval first, and get this approval in writing. This process can prove highly time consuming and laborious, but is absolutely vital if you don't want to end up falling foul of your best customer. An administration assistant can manage the overall process, but a senior member of the team may have to step in if the material seems to have got stuck in your customer's in-tray.

Photo library

A photo library is another administrative responsibility, and once it is set up you may find it a useful way of managing all the various photos that you've generated as the by-product of other marketing activities. Whenever a photograph is issued with a press release or article, a few extra copies should be stored in the library, cross-referenced to the press release with which they were originally used. As a result, the library will soon become a useful source of images which can be used in newsletters, articles, and to supply to any journalists who have mislaid original copies. If the library starts to get quite large, then one option is to scan all the images onto a CD-ROM for easier searching.

Monitoring response and evaluation

In Chapter 11 we look more closely at the different ways in which a PR campaign can be evaluated, and as you'll see, there are a number of different activities which can be undertaken. However, they all depend upon efficient administration – that press cuttings have been logged and filed correctly, that all journalist calls have been recorded, that feedback forms have been dealt with appropriately. It's also the job of your admin team to turn all this information into a summary of results which can be presented at the regular PR meeting.

Exercise

You are a PR consultant fully versed in all the best-known media liaison techniques. What would you advise in the following situations?:

■ The MD of a meat packing company wants to state his opinion on recent changes to export law.
■ A marketing department wants to promote the launch of a new model of mini bus.
■ A newly appointed sales director has just finished recruiting five new members to his team.
■ A major bank has just adopted the Klippit system in all its local branches.

PR Matrix

Time to add another column, this time entitled 'Activity'. Look at your audiences and messages and decide which can be best put across by the sort of media liaison activities we have been looking at in this chapter. We'll be adding other activities to this list in due course, so don't worry if you have large gaps at this stage – but you should find that there will be some media work that can be done for every audience on your list.

4 | COMMUNICATING DIRECTLY WITH A TARGET AUDIENCE

In Chapter 3 we looked in some detail at media liaison, which many people think of as the only type of PR activity. But there will be many occasions when it is vital that certain messages, or specific information reaches your target audience intact, and to rely on media coverage alone simply isn't enough. There will also be many situations in which you'll have a chance to meet target groups face to face and so you need to be prepared to make the most of such opportunities.

PR can help provide a strategic direction for direct communication, ensuring target groups receive information in the most appropriate way, making sure messages remain consistent and that they are transmitted using a variety of mechanisms in order to ensure maximum impact.

When to use direct communication

There are a number of situations in which direct communication is the best, and often most effective, option:

When the target audience is small and discrete

Often a key target group comprises only a handful of individuals. Possibly they are highly influential – perhaps they perform a specific role within an industry, and your marketing or PR analysis has identified them as being of key importance, not only for the power and influence which they wield, but also for the respect in which their views are held. Such 'key influencers' are always an important audience to target, and although they will (hopefully) take notice of any press coverage you generate, a more direct, precisely targeted approach will also prove worthwhile.

Even if the audience is not so influential, if it is small, and its needs are relatively specific then direct contact will certainly be a more efficient way of getting a message across. Use of direct mechanisms enable you to tailor your information to the interests of the group, and so deliver material which is more relevant and of better quality.

When you need to communicate a highly precise message

You can't rely on the media to transmit your every piece of news and, in many cases, what you consider to be news – although possibly of great interest to your target audience – won't merit media coverage anyway. Diary dates for example for seminars or exhibitions, minor product enhancements, or changes to a sales team – all useful information, but much easier to transmit directly, when you can be sure the information has been received. That is not to say that more important news shouldn't also be treated in this fashion – stories such as financial results, important technical changes or organizational restructuring will probably be covered by core media but possibly not in the detail crucial to a full appreciation of the story and its implications. Once again, direct contact – riding on the back of press coverage – can fill in the gaps and ensure complete understanding.

As a means of making regular contact

Regular communication is always important – especially if you are marketing a service, and there is no product on the shelf to promote your company for you. Advertising, media coverage, direct mail will all work together to provide a regular shop window for your organization, and regular, direct communication activities will all help to maintain a constant stream of news and information, increasing recognition of your organization even if its services are not being used.

When your audience is directly in front of you!

If you exhibit regularly at trade fairs or exhibitions, present seminars or attend industry conferences, then PR can be used to exploit your physical presence at the event. There are many specific PR opportunities that exhibition organizers provide, and it's important to take advantage of as many of these as possible.

To improve the effectiveness of distributors or agents

Although any remote sales force working on your behalf will be managed by your sales team, PR can play an important role in ensuring that strategic and consistent *communication* is maintained. One of the commonest complaints made by distributors or representatives is that they feel somehow out of the loop when it comes to hearing about developments within your organization. PR can help formalize the mechanisms by which such general information is transmitted to your sales force, wherever they are, helping them to feel more involved and ultimately enabling them to work more effectively on your behalf.

Direct communication – activities

Let's look at some tried and tested ideas for communicating directly with your key target groups:

Newsletters and magazines

Newsletters – whether produced in print, online or on CD – are everywhere. And despite complaints that they seem to proliferate needlessly, every organization still seems to need one. In fact, their very ubiquity can undermine their usefulness, so careful consideration of every aspect of content and production needs to be made in order to ensure that the end result is worth the effort and cost.

Why produce a newsletter? Well, it's a very good way of gathering together a wide range of information and by doing so demonstrate the full spectrum of activities that your organization undertakes. If you operate across a range of different business areas or have a number of initiatives running concurrently, then you can use the newsletter as a cross-promotional tool. It can highlight activities which customers may not be aware of, underlining the versatility of your organization and possibly encouraging use of, or interest in, other areas of your activity. They are also a good way of keeping people up to date with corporate news – new contracts, new appointments and so on. If your industry is one in which personalities are important (often the case in service industries or consultancies) then newsletters can be used to effectively profile individuals, or show how versatile staff can be – reporting on unusual hobbies or achievements outside work for example.

Increasingly, magazines are also being produced, often in tandem with a more regular newsletter. Sometimes quite glossy affairs, magazines often accompany a major document such as an annual report, and have quite high production values. Magazines represent a significant jump in both budget and production time (and headaches!) and so should only be considered if you think that the end result will really be worth the effort.

So what do you need to consider when planning a newsletter or magazine?

Frequency

Newsletters are much more effective if they are issued regularly. Frequency depends on a number of factors, but resources and budget will probably be two of the most important, as well as the matter of generating sufficient content. If your plans are fairly modest, then three issues per year is often a good number, to be distributed in September (when people are back at their desks after the summer), January or February (after the Christmas break) and then late spring. Avoid the main summer period, which is often quite a dead time, and make sure your dispatch schedule doesn't run into other major holidays such as Easter.

Magazines are not expected to be delivered with such regularity, unless you are a particularly large organization with a lot of news and views. Annual publication is often considered sufficient.

Content

When planning the content of your newsletter make sure that you don't just grab thankfully at any available material. Your newsletter will only ever be as good as the material it contains, so try to keep an editorial plan in mind, considering issues such as:

- Who is the newsletter for? Back to target audience again. Most organizations produce a single newsletter which is circulated to virtually everyone on their target list, as the news featured is of general interest to readers of all types. But if your audiences are large, and have a different range of interests or issues, then more targeted newsletters may be worth considering – a newsletter for customers, for example, would be very different from a staff or distributor newsletter. Keep your target audiences in mind throughout the rest of your planning process.

- How big is the newsletter? A fairly basic point, but at the top of your agenda must be an awareness of the amount of space you've got to fill. Once your design is in place (see below) you'll have a good idea of the average number of words needed to fill a page (remembering to allow room for headlines and photos). You can then decide the balance of copy on each page (which news will merit a full article, which can be presented as a snippet and so on), and write your text accordingly.

- Are all sections of your organization getting fair coverage? Do you need to give each team, division or group a section of their own, or should you devote a special feature per issue to each in turn? Consider your decision in the light of your marketing and PR aims – should you focus on your most profitable divisions? Which areas of your business can generate the most interesting copy?

- What *news* should you include? Review what has happened to your organization since the last edition, and identify any press releases which can be recycled, and those stories which have to be written from scratch.

- How should you balance the copy? Decide how you want to divide up the space you've got between news, case histories, opinion articles and so on. What should you put on the front page?

■ What regular items do you need to include? These could be diary dates, appointments, or business news for example, or even a regular 'thought piece' or profile of a member of your team.

■ What will happen during the time this issue is current? Will any conferences, product launches or other important events take place? Should you promote anything in advance?

■ Have you included the correct contact details? (Don't forget your web site address, and contact information for any regional offices if relevant.)

Generating copy can prove to be the hardest part of the whole process, but make sure that your editorial assessment is made on the basis of the needs of your readership, not just on whatever you can scrape together by the deadline! Remember that content can include discursive or opinion pieces as well as straight company or product news – some organizations even pay staff if they submit an article which is worth publishing, so that's also a tactic worth considering. It's a good idea to invite staff to contribute suggestions for content – this encourages a feeling of ownership amongst everyone within your organization, and counteracts any complaints if the next issue does not cover the work of a specific team in any great detail.

Don't forget illustrations as well – not all articles will need an accompanying photo or diagram, but you will need something on every page to add visual interest. If you don't have anything suitable, you may be able to use a royalty or copyright-free image, or else you can 'hire' images from photo libraries if you have the budget.

Once again, writing copy for a newsletter is a distinct skill and many organizations hire the services of a professional copywriter to both help them in their editorial decision-making, and to produce copy which is the right length for the space available, which strikes the right note, and which retains a consistency of style throughout the publication.

Design

It's important that a newsletter has a distinct identity, placing it apart from other forms of literature produced by your organization, and from newsletters produced by others in your field. A title will be needed, and a masthead (the title design, which sits at the top of the front page), and you should also create a template – a standard layout – which can be used for all pages and for all subsequent editions. Make sure the template remains sufficiently flexible so that the end result appears lively and interesting, not too rigid or wordy, and with plenty of opportunity to include a variety of illustrations. Unless you have in-house design expertise the use of a professional designer, experienced in newsletter production, is essential. Despite the availability of good dtp packages, design is a skill which cannot be acquired simply by sitting in front of a screen. A designer can also enlist the help of a copywriter, if needed, and oversee print and delivery, although obviously the management time involved will add to the cost. You can always ask a designer to create a masthead and template as a one-off job, and then arrange design, print and delivery yourself.

You also need to decide whether or not you want to use full colour – and once again, your budget will decide this for you. If you can't afford full colour, then black and white is not the only alternative, and a good designer will be able to suggest a number of options such as the use of coloured or textured paper, the use of spot colour (that is black and white and one other colour, used for effect), or the use of colours other than black – blue and white, for example or green and white, or three colours, perhaps exploiting any strong colours used in your logo.

Developing this last point, it is important that the newsletter, although having a discrete identity of its own, sits happily with other items of literature you may already have in circulation. If you are preparing a bundle of information for a visitor, then the more coherent it all looks when placed together, the more professional the impression. Let your designer see what other items you've already produced and make sure their appearance guides subsequent design ideas.

Also, tell the designer how the newsletter is going to be used – if it's primarily for direct mail, then the physical size is important, especially if you want it to fit into a standard envelope. A4 is by far the most common size, but A3 is often used, as is a tabloid format.

Print run and distribution

How many to print? Remember that newsletters have a limited shelf life so don't go overboard, but even so it won't take long for you to draw up a fairly sizeable basic mailing list. There will be your customers or contacts, then your advisers, suppliers, trade bodies and other such organizations, and you may need extra supplies for exhibition stands, your reception area and other venues which may be happy to hold a supply. You can add selected journalists to your distribution list, if they have already expressed an interest in your organization. Make sure that you can physically cope with the necessary distribution of the newsletter or use a mailing house if the whole process could prove to be too overwhelming.

Newsletters are very easy to print, so don't be afraid of approaching even the smallest local printer for a quote – or your designer can handle this for you. The most important factor, as far as you're concerned, will be the ability to deliver on time.

Feedback

Once the newsletter has been issued, it would be nice to know how it's been received. Often, the mere fact that you have managed to get something into the in-tray of every member of your target audience is success enough, and as newsletters are not designed as overt selling tools then achieving more than this really is a bonus. However, if you build in enough opportunities for direct feedback – e.mail addresses for brochures or more information, for example, or links to longer articles published on your web site (and we'll look at the use of the web later in this chapter) then you can start to get a feel for how well the newsletter has performed. Don't forget to include straightforward telephone and address details at the end of every newsletter – design a standard box which can simply be dropped into the last page of any design.

Once a year or so, you could insert a brief questionnaire into the newsletter, inviting general comment and specific feedback, and which could also be used as a means of cleaning your mailing list. However, the addition of an incentive (entry into a prize draw, or a pen or voucher for all who respond) can increase response significantly (not surprisingly!). If you plan to implement a PR

Audit (see page 18) then obviously use the exercise as a means of determining the usefulness or otherwise of the newsletter, especially when compared to other newsletters your target groups may receive.

Production schedule

Once you've decided to go ahead with a newsletter, then draw up a production schedule in order to make sure that every stage is given sufficient time. Work backwards from your ideal delivery date, and always allow extra time at each stage in order to cope with the unexpected. The final schedule will depend greatly on the number of pages you intend to prepare, but the following – for a four-page newsletter, with a print run of five thousand – will give you some idea of the timescales involved:

Weeks one to two
- Gather together background material for copy and brief team members if extra material is needed or interviews have to be set up
- Source illustrations
- Brief the copywriter
- Write copy

Week three
- First draft copy returned
- Circulate for comments and return to copywriter for amendments

Week four
- Second draft copy returned
- Circulate for final approval

Week five
- Approvals returned
- Pass to designer

Week six
- First design proof returned
- Circulate for approval to marketing team only

Week seven
- Design approved and finished
- Pass to printer

Week eight
- Delivery from printer
- Dispatch to mailing list

So as you'll gather, it's a two-month process for a simple four-page newsletter – although if the source material is complete, and your internal approval loop is limited then you can shave some time off here and there. If much of your material is coming from external sources, or approvals need to be gained from third parties, then you may find the whole process takes longer.

However, once you've been through the cycle one or two times you'll find that the routine becomes more automatic, and you'll also be able to better identify and plan for any 'milestones' – points at which the process goes out of your control.

Web sites

Most organizations now have a presence on the web and if they don't, then they all think they should. If you have a web site then it can play an active role within your PR strategy on a number of levels:

- as a major channel of communication (and therefore subject to the same checks and controls as are applied throughout your PR and communications strategy);
- as a place to publish latest press releases (see page 31 for more on the use of 'virtual press offices');
- as a way of promoting PR activities;
- as a repository for other forms of corporate communication such as your company profile, case studies and brochure text;
- as a vital element within a crisis management strategy (see Chapter 8 for more on this).

As you read through this book, you'll find reference to the use of web sites in virtually all the different PR activities covered.

For all its benefits, the web still remains a rather passive medium. Although you can – and should – put effort into directing visitors to your site, you depend upon your audience to search for information, rather than presenting the information up front, as you can with a newsletter. The web also demands the dedicated time of the user, taking them away from what they are doing and interrupting any other screen-based job they may be undertaking, whilst a newsletter can be used in a less deliberate way – glanced at quickly over coffee, for example, or read on the train.

Rather than rely primarily on the web and publish information exclusively there, instead look for ways to link your web site into other promotional activities, to encourage your targets to visit the site and find out more.

'Positioning papers'

If you have strong views about a certain issue, or you want to become known as a 'leading voice' on a developing trend, then a 'positioning paper' may well be a good vehicle in which to put your points across, and clearly state your opinion on the matter in hand.

Positioning papers usually adopt a simple format – they are not designed to be glossy brochures, but to be serious and thought-provoking. Quality of subject matter and writing is vital, and larger organizations often commission well-known journalists to prepare the copy, even giving them a by-line which in turn adds extra weight to the whole piece.

Positioning papers are a good way of demonstrating expertise within your organization and of providing target audiences with high quality information which they themselves may find invaluable when researching a particular issue. Such papers are also useful to send to journalists, to promote your organization's knowledge of a certain area, and hopefully to encourage more direct contact at a later date. High quality material is also welcomed by journalists as a resource they can draw upon if the subject matter arises at a more general level.

Corporate profile

A brief summary of your organization and the way it operates is a 'must-have'. You may already have a corporate brochure, but brochures tend to be promotional by definition, aiming to convey both information and image – they are also expensive to produce and so circulation will be tightly controlled. A corporate profile is a simple statement of fact, produced in the same way as a press release, and can be used to provide background information for journalists, as a page on your web site, or to be sent to anyone wanting some general details.

As a comprehensive summary of corporate facts and figures, a corporate profile should include the following information:

- The official name of your organization, and its relationship with any major groups or other bodies.
- Where it is situated (or where all its offices can be found).
- The number of employees (approximately – this number is always shifting).
- What it does – a summary of the raison d'être.
- How long it has been doing it for, plus any other pertinent historical facts which might be of interest.
- Its operational structure, giving names of the most senior executives/managers.
- Any financial information you can give.

As you begin to draft your own you'll no doubt think of other information which could be included – that's fine, but the final piece should be no more than one side of A4, as it should act as an instant source of information for anyone using it.

Exhibition support

Anyone who has ever had anything to do with a trade show or exhibition knows just how expensive they can be and how time-consuming to organize, and so it's important that you milk all possible publicity opportunities. PR is an ideal mechanism for exploiting the high profile exposure that an exhibition stand can bring, and so preparing a mini-PR campaign well ahead of the exhibition opening day is a good idea. (Note that exhibitions and conferences are also ideal opportunities for seminars and for public speaking – these two activities are given specific coverage later in this chapter.) When putting your PR plan together, make a checklist including the following ideas:

Planned opportunities

The exhibition organizer will provide a handbook or information pack which will detail all the PR opportunities generated on behalf of the event, and which you can exploit. These will range from the basic free entry in the show catalogue, to expensive sponsorship opportunities – you'll have to judge how much money you want to spend and how much impact you need to make. With specific regard to sponsorship, if you want to take advantage of some of the most high profile – sponsoring a keynote address for example, or an opening night drinks party – you'll have to be quick off the mark. Often they are booked as soon as the previous year's event closes, but many of the smaller opportunities – sponsoring publicity material for example – will remain an option until nearer the opening day. See Chapter 5 for more on how to assess sponsorship options.

Pre-show and post-show media coverage

If the exhibition is a major event, then all the main trade papers will cover it in some depth, and many will run preview features ahead of the opening day. Make sure you know the deadlines for these, and issue a press release announcing your stand number, and the main reasons why delegates should come and visit – issue a photo along with the release if you can. Send an adapted version of the release to all the magazines which only cover the event after it has happened, again with a photo if possible – don't attempt a shot of the stand, unless the stand design is exceptionally arresting. Most stand shots are at best generally illustrative, and it will be hard to identify the products or services that you are really trying to promote.

Check to see if radio or TV will be in attendance at the show and send an adapted release to the relevant stations, making the most of any audio or visual highlights which could attract a journalist to your stand.

Press-packs

Most exhibitions reserve a special room for the press, and exhibitors will be invited to provide press packs for display. In theory, only journalists will enter the room and take away relevant information – in practice, press packs can disappear with amazing speed, and one wonders if it's really the press or one's competitors who have benefited from the free supply of information!

Press packs are important, however, and although a limited supply should be available in the press room, it's a better idea to keep some on the stand itself, to hand to any journalist who might be passing or to give to those you've specifically arranged to meet.

A press pack should include:

- a general round-up press release, similar to the pre-show release already issued but obviously in the present tense;
- if necessary, individual releases on the specific stories promoted at the show, new products, new services for example, or new technologies;
- technical data sheets if necessary (single sheets providing technical background information);
- photographs, as appropriate;
- a company profile;
- a brief range of relevant company literature.

Press preview events

Some exhibitions hold press preview evenings, to which the media are invited in order to get their stories in advance, avoiding the crush of the opening day. Make the most of such opportunities – make sure you have plenty of press packs to hand, plenty of refreshments, and that you have enough staff on the stand to be able to provide information and answers. It's no use if all the media visiting your stand have to wait until they can talk to one individual. They will simply lose interest and wander off.

Media invitations

You'll be given a supply of invitations ready to be mailed to your target customer list, but save some for key press contacts and send them out together with your pre-show press release. If there is a press preview event, then make sure they know that you will be taking part. You may also want to get in touch with particularly good press contacts and invite them to make an appointment to visit the stand at a time apart from the other media, when they will be able to talk in peace to key individuals. It's worth chasing up such invitations by phone, as journalists will be inundated with similar requests.

On- and off-stand promotions

An exhibition is a great opportunity to offer corporate hospitality, or to take advantage of any seminar or conference programme that may be running in parallel with the main event. Rooms will often be available in which to host drinks receptions or buffet lunches for key contacts (including press) or for the general delegate crowd, and there may be opportunities to host a seminar or provide a speaker. See Chapter 6 for more on corporate hospitality, and how to make the most of opportunities to entertain.

On-going publicity opportunities

Publicity opportunities will continue even whilst the exhibition is in progress – make sure you know exactly what the organizers have planned so that you take advantage of opportunities such as 'show dailies' (a daily 'newspaper' published whilst the event is running), bulletin boards, dedicated radio stations, or publicity in the local daily paper. This is even more important if you yourself are having daily 'events' running on your stand.

Post-show

Tempting though it may be to issue a press release announcing that you had the best show in the history of your organization, it is unlikely to be used. The exhibition will be old news by the time the next issue of your target publication has been put to bed. However, it will be worth posting press packs to any of the most important contacts who you didn't manage to meet whilst the show was going on, especially if you've just had a launch event as part of the exhibition.

Seminars and roadshows

Seminars and roadshows are a popular PR tool, especially when the messages you want to convey are either quite precise, quite complex or simply informative, and the audience you want to target is well defined.

For the purposes of this chapter, a seminar is a one-off event (although it could form part of a series of events on a related theme), whereas a roadshow is the literal transportation of a seminar, presentation or even just an exhibition or display to a number of different locations around the country. A seminar can be run on a relatively small budget (compared to the budget for an exhibition, for example) yet can generate significant results. A roadshow is more complex to organize and expensive to stage, but once again the results can be impressive.

Seminars and roadshows can prove highly effective in a number of different ways, providing:

- an opportunity to mailshot new and existing contacts with information about the forthcoming event, raising profile without overtly 'selling' something;
- a chance to promote your organization to a focused, sympathetic audience;
- a good networking opportunity – you will find that many of your guests will often view a seminar or roadshow as an opportunity to network with both your staff and with other business contacts, so making them even better attended;
- a chance to mix satisfied clients with potential new clients within the same venue;
- a chance to meet contacts face to face, within a positive environment;
- an opportunity to generate new business;
- regarding roadshows in particular – an opportunity to generate sustained exposure for both your organization and the messages the roadshow (in particular) embodies.

Planning a seminar

Once again, good, strategic planning is the key to success. The following list provides some basic guidelines:

What to talk about?

Subject matter can be as wide-ranging or as specific as you want – and will be guided by the nature of the audience you hope to attract. General, issue-based seminars are a good idea if you simply want to use the event as a general awareness raising exercise. General seminars can appear more impartial, and therefore more authoritative – they can also tackle controversial issues, thus providing more opportunities for press coverage. More specifically targeted seminars, such as those linked to 'continuing professional development' can also be well attended, but by a highly precise group, and if this serves your purpose better then these will certainly reap better quality results than events where the audience has a less well-defined profile. Highly specific seminars also serve to showcase your specialist expertise, and raise the reputation of your organization as having the authority to speak on a certain issue. A last point on content – if you only want individuals of a certain level of seniority to attend, then make this clear both in your promotional material but also in the nature of the subject matter, and set the level of debate accordingly.

Encouraging interest

Obviously, the people you invite will know that you are not organizing such an event out of the kindness of your corporate hearts, but there are other ways in which you can attract their attention. Inviting independent speakers to join the presentation panel can prove very effective – or you could even co-host the whole event with a complementary organization. The press, from national dailies to local press, often co-host seminars and other events – after all, they are gaining exposure as well as your organization – and such co-operation can reap a whole range of promotional advantages, as well as guaranteed free publicity for the event itself. The only disadvantage will be the reluctance of other competing media to publicise the event, so if you do decide to approach a media contact with such an idea, make sure that they are the ideal partner and will generate sufficient publicity in order to ensure the event is a success.

Organization

A seminar is a major presentation, and there is a range of books that cover this topic in more detail (*Teach Yourself Business Presentations*, for example). See also the section on organizing a press conference for more ideas. However, when running a seminar as part of the PR campaign, the following points need to be considered, for example:

- ■ Make sure the whole event can be fitted comfortably into half a day: give guests refreshments on arrival, present the seminar, and then offer more extensive refreshments afterwards. Remember that networking is often as important as the event itself, so make sure you create plenty of opportunities for people to circulate and talk.

- ■ Confirm your guest list once your subject matter has been decided: don't forget to include your main business contacts, current and potential clients, suppliers, and the media. If you are inviting outside speakers, or working together with another organization, use this opportunity to exploit their mailing lists in order to make new contacts.

- ■ Decide if you want to open up the seminar, or to control attendance by issuing invitations. The former will of course generate widespread interest, and hopefully unearth brand new contacts, but runs the risk of diluting the audience with delegates from organizations or industries outside your target groups. The latter will produce a higher quality result, but promotional activity will be restricted, and of course the guests will already be mainly known to you, unless you buy in a list of likely contacts especially for the occasion. Of course, even if the event is open to all, you can still mail specific invitations to those people who you really want to come.

■ If you are planning an 'open' seminar then it's probably a good idea to charge for tickets. Don't consider this an immediate disincentive – a small charge will not put off serious delegates, but will certainly discourage freeloaders. Payment also confirms numbers, making catering and other arrangements easier to manage. If you still feel uneasy about the concept of charging entry to a PR event, then make it clear that all entry fees will go to a suitable charity.

■ The total number of delegates will depend on the size of the venue – which will in turn depend upon the numbers you hope to invite. If the invitations indicate that places may be limited then responses may be prompt. If response is overwhelming, quickly arrange another seminar to handle the additional interest.

■ Invitations should be clear, informative and visually interesting, and provide an opportunity for those unable to attend to request more information. A reply mechanism (email link, fax-back form or postage paid reply envelope) must be included, along with a map of the venue and instructions on how to reach it. As well as detailing the topic of the seminar, and a brief timetable to indicate running order, the invitation should also give more information on those slated to present.

■ Issue invitations six to eight weeks ahead of the seminar date. A telechase of key delegates can be instigated if pick up is slow.

■ Print your logo or the name of your organization onto pens or pencils and pads of paper which can be left on the delegates' chairs.

■ When selecting a venue choose a central location, easily accessible by road or train, and with ample parking. The novelty of the location will be of less importance than the nature of the seminar, but try to find a venue with a good reputation for handling such events. A good venue also positively attracts delegates so keep this in mind when considering your options.

■ Your guests will be expecting to leave with something, so make sure you prepare at the very least a wallet of information comprising: further information on the topic being discussed (i.e. leaflets, brochures, case histories, technical datasheets); potted biographies of any speakers; background information on your organization, including contact details; information on related topics.

PR activities to support a seminar

A seminar is 'news' in its own right, and should be promoted as such. If you have decided to run an open seminar then the local press and key trade media will probably be the most relevant to target, so aim to get at least a mention in a diary column, if not in the main editorial. Diary date information can be issued twice – once to make a general announcement, and then again to say that tickets are selling fast. When drafting your press releases, give all the necessary details about the event – date, time, venue and so on, but also stress any interesting or controversial aspects that will attract attention – the subject matter for example, or a well-known speaker.

Post-event publicity should always be considered, especially for invitation-only events, and even more so if a well-known speaker presented. Make sure you take plenty of photos of the event as it progresses, and prepare a press release to announce how successful the seminar was, issuing the release as quickly as possible after the event. If the subject matter was controversial, then that in itself could also become the subject of a press release, especially if a quote could be given as coming from an independent speaker. Offer transcripts of the speeches to the media, for use as articles (if you plan to do this, then make sure someone has made a note of the speech, or that it has been written down beforehand).

You could even offer coverage of the seminar to journalists as an exclusive, if you think that the subject matter and speakers are sufficiently enticing.

Roadshows

A roadshow is the repeated staging of a seminar, presentation, display or exhibition at different venues around the country. Roadshows are ideal if your audiences are geographically widespread, and if direct contact with as many as possible will reap real benefits, which is why they often form part of a consumer campaign. Many in the regions are irritated by the constant use of major cities as a focus for promotional events, and so the arrival of a roadshow closer to home may provide surprisingly popular. A media campaign needs be implemented at both national and local levels in order to promote the roadshow and encourage attendance – press releases, short syndicated articles, advertorials and promotions such as competitions and giveaways could be organized to coincide with your arrival at a specific venue.

A very wide range of options exists for roadshows, from a simple exhibition stand taken around the reception areas of selected business parks, to a fully fledged, truck mounted display, visiting as many venues as possible. Given all the possibilities a roadshow represents it's hard to offer general advice – one thing that is common to all travelling promotions is that they are very hard work, can be expensive, and can also generate a very high level of feedback which you will have to be prepared to deal with whilst the roadshow is running, rather than wait for the roadshow to complete its tour and return to base. You need to be sure the cost and effort will justify the results, and if you are unsure about how to tackle the whole concept, then approach a firm which specializes in such events and will help you both creatively and logistically.

Public speaking

How often have you listened to a speaker at an industry event and thought 'I could have done that!' or 'How did they get asked to speak to this audience?' Well, it's not all luck – public speaking opportunities are often a deliberate part of a PR strategy especially if your strategy includes the following aims:

■ The need to demonstrate industry knowledge and expertise.

- The need to exploit and capitalize on the reputation of key individuals.
- The desire to become a leading 'voice' within an industry or on a certain issue.

Public speaking opportunities should never be turned down without serious consideration, for they bring a wide range of benefits including:

- The opportunity to address a captive audience on an issue close to your heart.
- The chance to promote your organization within a 'neutral' environment – you have been invited to speak, rather than engineering the event yourself and so you will be regarded as an expert, rather than giving a corporate puff.
- The chance to make a direct impact upon an interested audience, one which may contain a range of new contacts.
- The opportunity to associate your organization with a particular set of values or issues, and raise its profile within a specific industry.

But also remember that public speaking has a few very specific drawbacks:

- It promotes the individual, sometimes at the expense of the organization. If you are a service industry for example, and one person gets particularly well known, then they will be the one every client asks for. If public speaking is to become a key activity, then make sure you field a number of different individuals in order to avoid 'personality PR'.
- Just as a speech can attract a lot of good publicity if everything goes well, it can also prove a disaster if things go badly. Make sure you minimize the risk by preparing as thoroughly as possible for the event, and banning the use of off-the-cuff remarks.

So how do you go about generating – and maximizing – public speaking opportunities? Draft an action plan based upon the following:

- Identify the issues or subjects upon which you want to talk, and about which you feel most knowledgeable – try to identify a mix of the factual, topical and controversial. As we've noted a number of times already, most industries have hot topics of the day and if you can add any new insights or expertise then these could be of great interest to a wider audience. Controversial speeches which challenge accepted wisdom, or cast doubts on an industry development will provide both an enticing item in a conference programme and also good copy for journalists.

- Identify all the likely conferences or exhibitions at which you could appear and get details of the conference organizers and any promotional agencies which may be handling programme arrangements. Many conference programmes are finalized months in advance, so make sure you contact the organizers as soon as you possibly can, if only to find out the date by which they need more information on your offer to speak. If you are a delegate at a suitable event, contact the organizers immediately afterwards to get more details about the next opportunity. You may also find that conference companies organize series of events, often on a similar theme, so ask them if they have any other opportunities which you could consider.

- Identify all the good speakers within your organization – there is no point fielding anyone who is either too inexperienced or too uncomfortable in such an exposed position. Make sure that even the most experienced presenters receive training at whatever level is appropriate, so that they are ready to present even unexpectedly – a lifesaver if a colleague suddenly has to cancel.

- Prepare a set of 'potted biographies' for the speakers you have identified, which can be mailed to conference organizers as further information, and which can also be used within programme notes or as handouts.

■ As you become better known, you'll find that you are asked directly if you can field a speaker – devise a proper response mechanism for such invitations. Before you accept, for example, make sure that the event in question reflects your overall aims, that the audience will include members of your main target groups, and that the surrounding event (if there is one) also provides valuable marketing opportunities. Make sure everyone in your organization knows that invitations to speak should be presented for general discussion – often invitations are the result of personal contact, but the opportunity needs to be evaluated carefully by the wider PR team, and accepted if at all possible.

■ Maximize any PR opportunities that speaking may offer: check to see if the organizers are issuing any press releases, and if not, issue one yourself; find out if photos are being taken, and if not, make sure you have a photographer on hand; find out if any media are being invited to the event, and mail them yourself with any additional information; offer your presentation script as a ready-made article to a relevant publication (although check first with the conference organizer).

Distributor/agent support

If you rely on distributors or agents to sell your products or services for you, then it's important that they remain as well disposed to you as possible, especially if you are only one of a number of organizations which they represent. Although the relationship with distributors will be handled primarily by your sales team, the degree to which this relationship remains successful and productive will depend upon the effectiveness of your communications – review all such forms of communication with your PR strategy in mind. For example:

Is contact formalized and regular?

You probably feel as though you're on the phone to them all the time, but how often is an unsolicited, 'how's it going' call made? Making sure such contact is timetabled as a regular activity can help improve communications greatly – you'll find that you are not constantly having 'problem-centred' conversations, and that both sides may find it more efficient to save up a number of different points to cover in one call rather than deal with each point individually. It will be up to you to decide how often such calls should be made – it can vary from once a week to once a month. The most important thing is that they are done, and a report of the conversation logged.

How is information disseminated?

Ensuring a regular flow of information is important, and the use of email and restricted access web sites has greatly increased the speed and ease with which such a flow can be managed and maintained. If your distribution network is extensive enough, then a newsletter may even be a viable option. Regularity is the key – make sure that whatever you decide to do, it's done regularly, even if it's just to report that there's not much to say!

Early warning

This can form part of either of the above activities, but it's an important issue to be aware of in its own right. You need to let distributors or agents know in advance of anything which might prove useful and which will help them to do their job more effectively, and especially of anything which may soon become public knowledge. This process is probably automatic when it comes to new products, product improvements or new services, but less so when it comes to marketing initiatives. It is important that they know if and when you are planning to issue a press release, for example, and for them to be aware of the distribution list. Not only will they then be able to gear up for additional customer interest, but they may also be able to capitalize upon it themselves by local promotional activities. They should also be copied in on the circulation of any good media coverage (especially local to their sales area), as they may be able to use the information in their own marketing – as a reprinted hand-out for example.

Template packs

Providing template press releases, newsletter layouts or general information sheets for your distributors or agents to use is another tactic to consider. These can be delivered via the internet, and stocks of paper carrying a simple background design, provided for instant reproduction.

The press release template can provide basic layout and content guidelines for a range of standard news releases (such as appointment news, contracts, sales figures etc.), Make it clear that these will be for local issue only so as not to clash with any national initiatives you may be planning. They are a good way of enabling your agents to take advantage of local opportunities for publicity, to which you may not have time or resources to respond, whilst allowing you to remain in control of content and style. Give advice on how to best use the material you are providing – many local distributors may have little experience of direct publicity, and especially of PR. If you know that some of your representatives are more PR-aware than others, then simply offer this as a service, and invite them to use it if they want to.

Events and entertaining

Entertaining always goes down well – your staff finally has a chance to meet and talk to contacts face to face, and your distributors or agents can meet a number of people at once, whilst also enjoying the benefits of your hospitality. The only drawback is the budget, which can mount up alarmingly especially if accommodation and travel costs are taken into account. To make the most of such events, try to tie them into other initiatives – a product launch for example, a trade exhibition, or a technical seminar, and add 'corporate hospitality' as part of the package. Regularity is again important – an annual event held at or near your headquarters is probably the minimum required, with additional events held regionally throughout the year.

Exercise

■ Draft an outline contents list for a four-page, quarterly newsletter for your organization.
■ List your current library of literature – sales, marketing, PR and other – are there any gaps which you can now identify and start to fill?

PR Matrix

Back to that activity column: would any of the activities we've discussed in this chapter be relevant to your audiences and messages? Add them in!

5 | SPONSORSHIP

Sponsorship is usually considered to be a more mainstream marketing activity, but it often falls within the PR remit because (a) it represents a form of high profile, non-overt communication and (b) usually generates a wide range of PR opportunities in its own right.

For many organizations, sponsorship is potentially a highly successful tool. It can create tangibility, in the form of an event, an occasion or a 'happening'; it can increase awareness among a target audience, maintaining this awareness in a variety of different media, and over a sustained period; and it can generate considerable goodwill for the sponsor from both target audiences and staff, both current and prospective. It can achieve all these things *providing* the process of sponsorship is managed strategically and evaluated properly.

For many charities, schools and a host of other organizations, commercial sponsorship is no longer the icing on the cake but a crucial part of the mix. As a result sponsorship opportunities are burgeoning as core funding is threatened – in fact, sponsorship is one of the world's fastest growing forms of PR or marketing activity, and so it's not so surprising that sponsorship opportunities sometimes seem endless.

Sponsorship could be defined as the art of corporate giving – in essence you are invited to make a contribution towards the running costs of an activity of some sort, and in return your name will be associated with that activity to a greater or lesser degree (depending upon the amount you pay). Sponsorship can be:

Exclusive

You are the only sponsor, gaining maximum exposure but also bearing all the costs. An exclusive sponsorship is worth considering if the audience is well defined, as there will be minimal wastage from your investment.

Joint

This is usually shared between complementary organizations (perhaps a conference co-sponsored by strategic business allies), or completely unconnected organizations linked only by their support for the organization sponsored, but you can find yourself co-sponsoring with direct competitors – this is usually the case for high profile events, such as major sporting occasions, where potential sponsors clamour to gain a slice of the sponsorship pie as any exposure is deemed worthwhile.

In kind

A less high profile, but some would say equally valuable form of sponsorship. Organizations are often invited to lend management or technical expertise to assist in the success of a particular event, or even in the ongoing running of an organization. Such sponsorship is common in the charitable and educational sector, and can prove very valuable to both the organization sponsored and to the staff who become involved in the scheme.

Why sponsor? Pros and cons?

Well-organized, accurately targeted sponsorship is a highly effective PR activity as it brings a range of distinct benefits:

Raised awareness among target audiences

Sponsorship is not designed to directly generate new sales leads or customers (although associated corporate hospitality may well do so), but it will increase overall awareness of your organization and its 'philosophy', underlined by the nature of the sponsored organization or event benefiting from your support.

Direct identification with your target audiences

This is particularly appropriate when promoting consumer products, but is also relevant to any organization considering a sponsorship opportunity. By sponsoring a certain activity you are saying to your audience, in effect, 'we like what you like' and are therefore attempting to create a 'bond', creating and enhancing the chemistry that is an essential part of the successful relationship with a target group. Remember that this works two ways – some audiences may positively dislike the object of your sponsorship, so be prepared to either live with their disenchantment, or to expand your programme to embrace a range of different sponsorships in order to appeal directly to different target groups.

Long-term, high-quality exposure

Events which run for a sustained period of time obviously offer extended benefits, but even one-off events offer a wealth of opportunities before and after the event has taken place. Sustained exposure is particularly useful for service organizations which need to continuously remind the market of their presence. If you don't want to embark upon a prolonged campaign, or haven't the resources to support it properly, then a viable alternative is to sponsor an annual event, such as an Award, a concert or competition, with which your name can become synonymous, enabling the sponsorship to work on your behalf even when promotional activities are not taking place.

Creating closer links between your organization and a 'strategic ally'

Joint sponsorship in particular reaps this specific benefit. We've already considered the idea of co-sponsoring a seminar with a key trade magazine – this is an ideal example of how joint sponsorship can reap even greater benefits than straightforward association. In fact, many sponsorships result from a deliberate aim of forging stronger links with a particular organization. Unexpected synergies can often result from co-sponsoring arrangements – especially if you are unfamiliar with your partners. You may even get some extra business yourself!

Improved image

Sponsoring a 'good cause' whether charitable, educational or artistic can serve to raise awareness of your organization's philanthropic approach, and civic responsibility. Knock-on effects can include goodwill from customers and staff, stronger ties with the local community – important if its support may be needed in the future – and increased respect among your peers. Association with a good cause can also add an element of 'character' to a possibly faceless organization, and may well provide a number of opportunities for employees to get involved in something beyond the scope of their everyday work.

Staff involvement and support

Sponsorship can be used as an informal element of staff development programmes, helping to develop skills such as team building, planning and project management. Staff can also benefit directly from sponsorship, through free tickets to an event for example; the association of one's employer with a high profile occasion can also help boost morale. Staff can even help direct the sponsorship programme, by highlighting opportunities or by voicing support for a specific cause. You may even find that some of your own staff – particularly amateur sports people – are an ideal vehicle for sponsorship.

A showcase, and testing ground, for expertise

This depends greatly on the nature of the sponsorship. For example, IT has a traditionally strong link with motor sport – a symbiotic sponsorship which provides racing teams with cutting-edge technologies and techniques, and IT companies with a high pressure, time-critical environment in which to hone skills, hardware and software. And as a result they have a global showcase for their technologies and expertise. On a less ambitious level, 'sponsorship in kind' could reap equally rewarding opportunities to demonstrate management or problem-solving skills.

But despite this impressive range of benefits, there are some significant disadvantages which must also be considered:

Expense

You get what you pay for – guaranteed high exposure will translate into high cost. An alternative, although riskier approach is to sponsor a less well-known event and then use PR to promote it to the hilt. Also, your initial budget may easily double by the end of the programme, if you add in your own promotional costs to cover activities such as a dedicated media relations campaign, advertising, corporate hospitality, direct mail, staff time and so on. Sponsorship alone will not make sufficient impact without additional marketing support.

Scatter-gun marketing

Although audience reach may be wide, the net effect can still be minimal. For example, high-profile sports sponsorship may be appealing in terms of the TV exposure gained, but what percentage of the audience is actually influenced by what is, in effect, covert TV advertising? A low key, but more highly focused event – perhaps a charity cricket match to which a large number of targets can be directly invited – may yield more tangible results.

High-profile success – high-profile disaster

If your involvement demands the supply of any sort of technology or service then it is essential that you perform as demanded or else you will become the focus of bad publicity and serious discontent. Likewise, if the event itself draws negative publicity (not mentioning any dome-like structures on the banks of the Thames) then you may suddenly find yourself associated with a disaster rather than a success, and for no fault of your own. Although more expensive or more controversial sponsorship opportunities may generate more publicity, tight management and control will be essential. A crisis management programme (see Chapter 8), established in advance, can prepare for possible damage limitation should things start to go wrong.

Overkill

Increased competition among sponsors, especially for highly popular, well-publicized events, has resulted in a greater division of opportunities as organizers, not surprisingly, aim to generate as much income as possible. The resulting proliferation of sponsors can cause media 'clutter' and confusion among target audiences, with only the top-spending sponsors rising above the noise. It can also result in such a small slice of the cake being available that the end result is negligible.

Cynicism

There is no point trying to pretend that any sponsorship deal you strike has been done purely out of philanthropy. It has been done because, (a) you had the money to spare, (b) you can see some benefit to be gained for your organization and (c) it meets the aims of your PR strategy. But if handled well, the end result need not appear too calculated, and the strong relationship between the sponsor and your organization can build into something that can remain positively beneficial for many years to come.

Developing a sponsorship programme

For most smaller organizations, sponsorship will so far have been a haphazard and opportunistic activity, perhaps only taking place at trade fairs, or focusing on local events which provide an opportunity for 'corporate hospitality'. If you want to think more seriously about sponsorship, then first outline the criteria to use when evaluating any future opportunities or when generating your own ideas. Consider:

- Your current marketing and PR strategy and aims and objectives, especially key audiences and messages.
- The broader areas of sponsorship that are most appropriate to both your corporate culture and that of your target audiences (see below for more on this).
- The budget you want to allocate.
- The activities of your competitors – can you compete effectively, is the field still wide open, or have certain opportunities already become firmly associated with another sponsor?
- How you plan to evaluate the success of the sponsorship, once in place (and we'll look at that in more detail at the end of this chapter).

Once you've outlined a broad brief, then you can start to consider the options open to you. Sometimes it may seem that almost anything that moves can be sponsored, and in the case of leading sports personalities, sponsored many times simultaneously. Ideas for sponsorship vehicles are often 'packaged' and presented to potential sponsors, but you can also think of ideas of your own, especially if you have a highly specific aim in mind.

To start you off, however, let's look in more detail at a few of the most popular sponsorship categories:

Sport

Sponsorship has become an established part of the sporting world, and opportunities range from your local school's sports day to the World Cup.

Advantages

Sports sponsorship has a long history and is therefore an established, safe and relatively easy option. Many major sporting events or organizations offer sponsorship opportunities, and have extensive experience in managing sponsors, their money and their expectations. Depending upon the chosen sport, sponsorship can also offer good opportunities for corporate hospitality at a generally pleasant, informal occasion. It can also generate very high-profile publicity – particularly in the broadcast media – and is often associated with business values such as competitiveness, endeavour and success. Sports sponsorship is often popular with staff, especially if they can take advantage of free tickets.

Disadvantages

A very wide variety of opportunities exist, but finding an exclusive deal is becoming both more difficult and more expensive. The cost of sponsoring even a small part of a high-profile sporting occasion can also be high, and yet you will still only gain minimal exposure.

The more traditional the sport, the more conservative the end result, and although this may suit certain target groups it may not provide any great differentiation for the sponsor, unless the sponsorship is particularly impressive or generous. In terms of corporate hospitality, there is also the risk that your guests may be jaded by the frequency of such events and therefore be less impressed by an invitation. It should also be noted that certain sports – such as tennis or cricket – appeal to a wider audience in terms of sex and age than football or Rugby, sports which can prove a positive disincentive to certain target groups.

Arts

Arts sponsorship has become increasingly high profile in recent years, and as a result increasingly well organized.

Advantages

Arts sponsorship can be as conservative or as radical as the sponsor desires, and is associated with imaginative and creative skills, as well as demonstrating taste and education. Many artistic events last over a period of time – an exhibition for example, or a programme of concerts – resulting in a string of associated opportunities (such as in-gallery entertaining) and long-term publicity. The philanthropic nature of arts sponsorship often reflects favourably upon an organization and it can often prove to be a less expensive option, and one that appeals to a very wide spectrum of people.

Disadvantages

The arts can be seen as elitist, and the events sponsored are often relatively low key. Resulting publicity may be less, and may only be gained in certain media. Many smaller artistic organizations are not as commercially aware as their sporting counterparts, and therefore more management time from the sponsor will be required to ensure the desired results are achieved.

Business-to-business

Opportunities are always available to sponsor Awards, events or competitions within the business community, either within your own industry or in 'vertical' markets – markets complementary to your own.

Advantages

High-profile publicity can be generated directly amongst a key target audience without much wastage. Business sponsorships are often joint affairs, allowing the sponsor to get closer to an organization which could be of use in the future – a trade association, for example, or again a key publication. Many sponsorship opportunities centre upon an annual event (in the case of an Award for example), and so the chances for repeat sponsorship are increased, with a greater degree of recognition being achieved each time. Business to business sponsorships tie your organization closely to a particular sector or regional community, and can also demonstrate active support for higher standards, or values such as excellence, performance and ambition.

Disadvantages

Once again, this is a very overcrowded area, and one in which many sponsorships are merely PR exercises, dreamt up to generate extra publicity – as a result they can appear contrived. Care is needed to ensure the sponsorship is worthwhile, and attracts the desired attention. Award programmes can backfire if no one enters, or if entries are of the wrong quality. They also demand extra management time in terms of administration and judging of entries.

Education

Sponsorship opportunities are available at all levels of the education system, from nursery school to postgraduate, and are increasing year by year.

Advantages

Fostering direct links with the education system can deliver a number of advantages: improved links with the local community; improved recruitment; the opportunity to raise awareness among students of your products or services – and parents as well. As schools and colleges clamour for better resources, the opportunities for sponsors to provide these resources are enormous, and many companies exist specifically to help organizations make the most of the education sector, providing guidance on how to link any activities directly to standards of educational achievement, or to meet specific classroom needs.

Disadvantages

Commercial sponsorship in the school system sometimes receives a lukewarm reception: although accepted as unavoidable, it is often criticized as disguised advertising and manipulation of a naive audience. If you attract negative publicity for any other aspect of your business this can also backfire on any educational sponsorships you may be supporting.

Involvement at the higher education level can be expensive and – as is the case in any training investment – is no guarantee that the skills or knowledge you aim to encourage will be used on behalf of the sponsoring organization. It is another very crowded market place, so promoting or differentiating the sponsorship will be difficult, unless it is particularly innovative.

Charitable or cause-related sponsorship

Although many of the organizations already considered – arts groups, sports clubs and so on – are already registered as charities, this section refers more to the 'good cause'. Corporate charitable giving has declined in recent years, as the evaluation of return has proved increasingly difficult to assess. Charities are well aware of this and have responded by increasing the range and sophistication of the opportunities available, enabling them to compete more effectively with more commercial organizations also battling for a share of the sponsorship pot.

Advantages

Depending on the nature of the charity, sponsorship can generate considerable publicity and goodwill, as well as providing an opportunity for staff involvement at all levels. Long-term relationships – and therefore exposure – are positively welcomed, and an organization can become closely associated with a good cause. It's also a good way of fostering closer links with a local community, if the direct benefits of the sponsorship (a mini-bus for example, or a community resource) can be easily appreciated. The choice of a 'good cause' which reflects the nature of an organization can also prove highly valuable – a major employer of female staff could choose to support a breast cancer charity, for example, or a manufacturer of optical products could support a charity working with the partially sighted.

Disadvantages

Opportunities in this area are legion – considerable care is needed when selecting a charity to support, and unless a considerable sum is donated in one direction, very little impact may be made. Sponsorship money may have to be regarded as pump-priming, and additional effort required in order to effect a more tangible and successful end result. Smaller, less well resourced charities will also need greater management input from the sponsor in order to ensure the smooth running of the relationship. Ending a sponsorship agreement can result in negative publicity unless managed carefully.

Managing the relationship

Sponsorship is not simply an act of handing over money – it needs to be managed effectively right from the start, beginning with a clear understanding of the expectations of both sides. Ensure that those members of your team who will be running the sponsorship are involved right from the start, in order to make sure everyone knows what is expected of them. The amount of management time you or your colleagues will need to donate must also be clearly laid down.

As was said earlier, many organizations are becoming increasingly sophisticated in the way they package their sponsorship opportunities, but even clear cut sponsorship agreements must be well defined in advance in order to avoid arguments down the line. For example, if your logo is to appear whenever a certain event is publicized, then make sure you know exactly how big the logo will be and how it will be used – in a muddle with everyone else's, or clearly on its own? If part of the deal promises corporate hospitality, check on how exclusive this will be – will you be able to entertain clients in your own room or marquee or will you simply be given a supply of free tickets? It's difficult to generalize, because every agreement is different, but it's important to iron out any ambiguities right from the start.

Once the sponsorship is up and running, maintaining contact is vital. You need to make sure that promised publicity has been organized, you'll want to check the use of your name in any promotional literature or press releases, and you'll want to get a feel for how successful the sponsorship is as soon as it starts to go 'live' – not least to help you plan and implement your own supporting PR campaigns. Book regular meetings for all involved, with a standard agenda in order to ensure all details are regularly reviewed – you'll want to publicize the sponsorship yourself in staff and customer newsletters, and so this meeting will be an ideal way of gaining progress reports.

Evaluation

Sponsorship – as for any broad-based marketing activity – is difficult to evaluate, but evaluation is nevertheless essential in order to ensure spend is maximized, and to establish whether the exercise is worth repeating as many sponsorship deals can last for a considerable amount of time – even years. The key to proper evaluation is the setting of realistic, measurable aims and objectives at the outset of the sponsorship agreement. Here are some examples of how to assess a range of different sponsorship aims:

- **Aim: increased awareness of your organization's name among key target groups.** Look at the concrete achievements, and the nature of the activities undertaken and assess their benefits: assess the frequency of any media coverage for example, and where it was gained and use your own best judgement to evaluate whether it really was working as hard as it could. If your exposure was only limited to a few posters placed in less than successful sites then you may have a right to question the impact your spend has achieved.

- **Aim: increased coverage in key media.** In Chapter 11 we look in more detail at the ways of assessing media coverage, and you can apply these methods to your sponsorship campaign, gaining a feel not only for how often your name was associated with the sponsorship, but also coverage of the sponsorship itself without your name being mentioned – this may give cause for concern, if you discover that your involvement was largely ignored.

■ **Aim: to increase links with the local community.** This is harder to assess, and will depend upon a combination of factors including local press coverage, local exposure in other ways, and the success or otherwise of the event which you were sponsoring. Have you found a greater awareness among current staff or new recruits of your 'presence' in the community? Have you received more direct approaches from other relevant local groups?

See Chapter 11 for more on all the different evaluation techniques that can be applied, and use them in this context.

Exercise

Once again, donning your PR consultant's hat, what type of sponsorships would you recommend for the following clients?:

■ A high street bank, with a traditional reputation, wanting to raise its profile within the local business community.

■ A high street bank with a reputation for modern ideas and new thinking, wanting to raise its profile within the hi-tech community nationwide.

■ The Clean Sweeps – wanting to raise its general profile among both prospective clients and add it to your list.

PR Matrix

Back to your activity column – could sponsorship provide some good results? See where it could be used and jot it down.

6 | ENTERTAINING AND CORPORATE HOSPITALITY

Many people think of PR as a combination of press work and cocktail parties but as I hope we have already demonstrated, nothing could be further from the truth. However, it has to be said that 'corporate entertainment' does usually fall under the remit of the PR department and it can form a very useful – and often very enjoyable – aspect of a PR campaign. Corporate entertaining can extend from a quick lunch down the pub, to a full weekend away for clients and their families, and from a small group event to an 'open house' party – with associated budgetary implications. And remember, entertaining should not just be aimed at your customers and contacts. Your staff and suppliers may also need rewarding, or given a chance to socialize informally. As ever, it's always better to plan strategically, and this goes for entertaining as much as for any other PR activity, even though the end result may be designed to appear spontaneous and unforced.

Before we start, however, let's look at the benefits of corporate entertaining in order to identify those which best suit your PR programme:

An opportunity to develop relationships

Any form of corporate entertaining aims to create an informal atmosphere in which you can get to know your guests better – whether they are important prospective clients or long-serving staff. This is especially valuable to service organizations, which place a high value on the 'chemistry' that often persuades a client to use one organization rather than another. Away from a 'hard-sell' environment, conversation can focus on topics other than business (and in fact business talk is often actively discouraged) and a convivial atmosphere, helped along by an attractive setting or interesting event, can help key relationships develop at a more fundamental level, paving the way for a stronger relationship in the future.

An opportunity to target a wide range of audiences

Other events organized as part of your PR programme have probably focused more closely on specific target audiences. Entertaining, without the work-related remit, can be used as an excuse to invite everyone on your target list, and get them together at the same time. The positive PR that can be generated by a mix of satisfied and potential customers is tremendous. And the mix of less obviously related groups – suppliers, for example, and support staff – can also lead to a much more interesting and fruitful end result.

As a way of saying 'thank you'

If your organization has been growing rapidly, then it's probably taken all your time and effort to keep on top of day to day developments. Corporate entertaining gives you the chance to stop and say 'thank you' to all the people who have helped you so far – once again, to customers, suppliers, staff – in fact to anyone who has supported your organization in the past and who you want to continue doing so in the future.

A night to remember!

Events organized under the banner of 'corporate entertaining' are often very popular – you should have no difficulty in filling all available places! The business community, especially a local business community, uses parties as yet another networking opportunity but as a result they can occur with increasing frequency so may find that you have to work harder to stand out from the crowd, especially if you want your event to be an occasion to remember and the quality of the guest list to remain high. You yourself may already have been invited to a range of different parties and events – which invitations did you accept and why? Why did you turn down others? Use your own experience to guide your initial thoughts, as it's likely that others invited to the same events represent at least some of your key target groups.

If you've decided that entertaining should become part of your PR plan then, once again, outline a strategy which will make the most of your budget. Use the following parameters to help you:

Who do you want to 'entertain'?

Make a wish list of all those who you think it would be beneficial to entertain: the list will probably include your most important clients and customers (former, current and potential), key contacts, major suppliers and distributors and, of course, your staff. Don't forget to include those 'key influencers', however, those who are vital to the running of your organization and who may also be able to recommend you to other potential contacts. Include your business advisers, your bank manager, your accountant and others such as management consultants, independent advisers and journalists. The list may now look rather frightening, but it's important to assess the range and scope of contacts you want to entertain – in fact, it may become clear at this stage that you need to consider a number of different options (especially if your ideal guest list is geographically widespread), rather than hold one big bash.

Of course, you can always entertain contacts on a one-to-one basis, but also look at ways in which you can band them together. If you think it's worth hosting an annual 'event' (and we'll look at the sort of thing you could do later in this chapter) then this would be an ideal way of entertaining all your 'A-list' contacts at once. As the cost of such events can prove quite high, you may not think it worth inviting your 'B-list' along, but instead make sure they are invited to events such as seminars, conferences or exhibitions, where hospitality is part of the occasion – once again, this will also enable you to entertain effectively around the country. You may also consider a less expensive option, such as a drinks party, as a better way to entertain such 'secondary contacts'.

How often do you need to entertain?

Once again, entertaining your target groups in a number of different ways, over the course of a year, may be more effective than simply holding one annual party. Your most important contacts may need to be entertained frequently – especially if you work in an industry which depends upon a few important contacts, and which exploits personal chemistry to help generate repeat business. For example, you probably take your clients out to lunch, but now is the time to make sure it's timetabled regularly. It starts to sound rather forced, but your clients need never know that you've allocated an annual entertainment budget of three trips to the pub and two smart lunches. Formalizing 'informal' contact in this way makes sure that you really do encourage the relationship, and also means that you spend the same amount of time with each contact – not just those that you get on well with!

What type of entertainment would suit the needs of your target groups?

Rather than the actual event, consider more the context. Issues such as the scale of the entertainment, the style, the atmosphere and so on. For example, if you need to entertain an important foreign visitor, then a trip to a sporting event could prove interesting, but rather than hire a marquee and invite all and sundry, keep the guest list to a minimum – yourself, your second in command, spouses and of course your guest and family. Such one-on-one attention would be completely inappropriate for staff, however – they will want to let their hair down and get well away from the work environment. Perhaps a day at an activity centre, riding quad bikes and tanks would prove more appealing? You may need to consider the seniority of your targets as well, considering how best to mix individual groups – an exclusive dinner will suit CEOs, for example, open house at a local pub would be ideal for new trainees.

What's your budget?

Now you know who you want to entertain, how often, and roughly in what way, you can start to sketch out exactly how much money could be involved – and you'll probably want to reduce it! Of course, this exercise depends greatly upon the size of your marketing budget, and just how beneficial you feel entertaining could be to your business. Make sure you timetable a budget review at the same time as you evaluate the success of the events you've been hosting, so that you can trim or expand the amount of money you allocate.

Choosing the right option

Money, as you'll now realize, can prove crucial to the success or otherwise of an event, especially a high-profile occasion. Cost can also raise other, more subtle issues. The last thing you want is for guests to go hungry or thirsty, but if the entertainment is lavish, will it appear *too* generous? If you are running a service company, will your clients think that you must be charging too much if you can afford to entertain on such a grand scale? Every scenario will be different, so you must use your skill and judgement to assess the impact of what you have in mind – if you are at least aware of these issues then you are more likely to avoid any unpleasant fall-out.

Despite the fear that you have to pull out all the stops, you can achieve good results without necessarily breaking the bank, so let's divide the options by cost in order to give you some ideas:

Low-cost

A trip to the pub is probably the cheapest way to entertain a client – and, ironically, can often be the most successful. If this becomes a regular activity, then start to build up a database of places that you know and trust, that can be relied upon to deliver efficient service in a pleasant atmosphere – and make sure you blacklist any that fail. There is nothing more embarrassing than having to wait ages for food that turns out to be indifferent. Pubs which offer both restaurant and bar meal options are good bets, especially those which will allow you to book in advance. A more formal meal can also be a relatively low-cost, but impressive, option especially if you suggest a restaurant with a very good reputation. Once again, at the risk of sounding mechanical, make a note of where you went, and make sure you don't return there every time – unless you are allowing your guest to choose.

Co-hosting an event can also help keep budgets low. If you want to have a drinks party, for example, you could find a complementary organization which may be happy to share the costs of a venue with you, although as most catering companies charge per head for food and wine your final budget will still relate directly to the numbers invited. Obviously, a shared event results in a less exclusive atmosphere, but the opportunity to mingle with groups of new contacts can have its advantages.

Add-on entertaining – associated with a seminar or exhibition for example – is a good way of maximizing both your promotional and entertainment budget. Your venue and invitation costs will already be accounted for within your presentation expenses, so the post-event finger buffet or drinks reception will be cost-effective in terms of both budget and effort. Such entertaining positively attracts delegates to seminars and the like, as they want to take advantage of the networking opportunities on offer, but guests will expect to talk more about business than to generally socialize.

Medium-cost

Medium-cost options include events such as exclusive lunch or drinks parties. As we've already noted, the final cost will depend upon the number of people you want to invite. The venue you choose will be important and will help attract people especially if it's a particularly pleasant or unusual place. Such events may work better if they are linked to a theme or an event, in order to give a raison d'être and context. The most obvious, of course, are those linked to seasonal celebrations: Christmas (but diary clashes will be inevitable), Pancake day, a summer garden party, bonfire night – you'll always be able to find some excuse. Alternatively, is there anything that your organization wishes to celebrate such as a corporate birthday (ideally a landmark such as ten or 25 years), or the opening of a new facility or building? As with any party, atmosphere is everything, and so you must try and ensure that the setting, the food and guests all combine to create a memorable event. As for all activities, party organizers can be called in if you think you need professional help. They are very useful when it comes to handling all the administrative details, which can be extremely time-consuming, and they have access to a wealth of contacts – they'll also be able to put forward a host of ideas to make your party go with a swing.

High-cost

If you are prepared to spend serious money, then you can organize a truly memorable occasion, and there are endless possibilities from which to choose – from front row seats at a major sporting event, to trips abroad, to hot air balloons, to your own sponsored horse-race, a truly lavish party – and a host of companies are ready and willing to spend your money for you and organize the whole thing from start to finish.

If you really do want to impress your key contacts, or perhaps reward your best distributors or employees, then an invitation to an exclusive or popular event can prove undeniably attractive. Tickets for the final at Wimbledon, a full day at Ascot – we can all think of examples. They will be expensive, but certainly will be a day to remember. If the occasion becomes a regular annual event, then it may even become in indirect means of encouraging loyalty and individuals will actively look forward to their annual invitation.

However, the 'PR jolly' – where the best seats are snapped up on behalf of people who don't really have an interest in what they are about to see – has earned the PR industry, and some of its clients, a rather unsavoury reputation. But as the reciprocal relationship between corporate entertainment and event management becomes ever more closely entwined, then the results are becoming accepted as a fact of life.

A few basic guidelines

As an event can be an expensive activity it's important to make the most of the opportunities you are creating. Although everyone will be having, hopefully, a good time, you will still have to work hard to make sure your basic aims are fulfilled. The following advice should help:

Plan meticulously

As with every other marketing and PR activity, planning is essential in order to ensure that everything goes smoothly, especially when the occasion is supposed to be relaxed and enjoyable. There are many companies which will handle the planning of such events for you, or which offer self-contained packages based on tickets to a sporting or other event, and which include refreshments and other diversions. Although expensive, such companies will take away the burden of detailed planning, which would otherwise have to be delegated to a member of your administrative team. They will also provide all the staff needed to run the event on the day, leaving you free to concentrate on your guests.

Make sure your event reflects your corporate ethos

This point echoes those made in the chapter on Sponsorship and it's worth saying again. You can use corporate entertaining to underline and strengthen your corporate image. For example, if you are operating in a 'traditional' and perhaps conservative market sector – business advice for example – then a wild party will suit neither your image nor your target audience, which will be expecting an invitation to a cricket match, or a concert. If it's important to stress your imaginative and creative abilities, then apply these to your choice of venue or type of event. Once again, events are supposed to be relaxed, informal and enjoyable so it's important that your audience does not feel uncomfortable by being placed in surroundings in which they feel unsure. Such events may also tie in nicely with any sponsorships you have embarked upon, to reinforce the point that you are supporting local sport or music for example.

Prepare to be entertaining!

Your guests will expect you to be a charming, courteous host throughout the event you've planned, so mentally prepare for a long stretch of smiling attentiveness! If you know that some of your clients can be hard-going socially, then make sure you have colleagues on hand to take over the reins at certain points. Broadening the invitation to include spouses and partners can help greatly in such circumstances, also increasing the informality and conviviality of the occasion. If you are planning a party, then make sure you invite an interesting mix of people, including some you know are always 'good value' – likewise, make sure that any employees attending can circulate with confidence and are not put off by a room full of people they don't really know. You must also manage a balancing act of talking to the people you really need to impress, whilst making sure that everyone is being attended to – once again, brief colleagues to make sure no guest is left alone.

Exercise

The Klippit company is now growing fast – it has a team of reps out on the road, a growing employee base and is now hunting for more investment in order to grow into the next stage. Should it be thinking about using entertainment as one of its strategic activities? Devise a plan of action, identifying the different events the MD could consider, the target groups which could be invited, and the benefits it would gain the company.

PR Matrix

Review your activity column once again – do you need to entertain any of your target groups? Add an appropriate activity to your list.

7 INTERNAL PUBLIC RELATIONS

When it comes to listing target audiences, staff are often somewhere near the bottom of the list – if they've been remembered at all. Yet your staff are one of the most important factors in the success of your organization especially if you are a service company, and stand or fall on the enthusiasm and loyalty of your employees. When all your other PR activities start falling into place, you'll start to raise the expectations but no matter how good your PR campaign may be, an organization will stand or fall on the actions of its staff. Unless they are as enthused as your customers or clients then the whole business structure can come crashing down. Internal PR can provide some of the glue which can bond an organization together.

An 'Internal Communications' strategy can be invaluable within your overall PR programme. No matter how few people you actually employ, it's surprising how quickly an individual can start to feel 'left out' of the general news round, even in an office of only three or four, simply because there is no formalized mechanism for internal communications. This problem can become worse if some of your staff (and many do) work from home or are part-time, or are simply often away from their desks. Implemented as part of your overall PR strategy, an internal PR campaign will help give structure to the process of communicating messages within your organization. But it shouldn't simply be regarded as a better way of sending memos – internal PR can also achieve some serious goals:

■ Spreading the concept of 'ownership' among staff at all levels, making them feel more involved. The feeling that management is operating an open policy towards information gives out a positive message to all employees.

- Encouraging staff involvement by creating mechanisms which enable staff to make suggestions and comments both informally and formally.
- Creating feedback mechanisms which are regular, sustained and accountable, and which show that staff are listened to – rather than simply encouraged to talk.
- Providing a greater sense of 'unity', especially if you operate from more than one office, have sites overseas, or a remote sales force or distributor network.
- Counteracting the spread of rumour, gossip and – by default – misunderstanding, by providing more information up front, and by disseminating it faster.

By definition, an internal PR plan needs to be management driven, led (and to a greater extent administered) from the top. So why commit valuable time to such a programme when it could be spent actively marketing your organization? Here are some of the benefits:

- Staff will become committed, active partners in the growth of the organization, feeling that their contribution has made a difference on more than one level.
- Clients will receive better service from all employees, if those employees feel more involved in their organization.
- Mechanisms are put in place for the efficient transmission of information of all types, both positive and negative – staff know where to go to find out information, and in the case of a crisis, such information can be disseminated quickly and efficiently. Rumour – and by default misinformation – will be kept to a minimum.
- Insecurities and bad feeling resulting from poor or no communication will be kept under control.
- Good suggestions made by any individual within your organization can be used for the benefit of the whole workforce.

For an internal communications campaign to be successful, however, it demands more than just the will of the PR team – you'll also need to ensure:

- Commitment from all levels of management – you can't afford to let one of your team leaders or directors opt out from the stated policy once it's put in place. If different staff receive different information, or information of different quality, then the outcome may be divisive and potentially damaging.
- That individuals at all levels of seniority are encouraged to listen as well as contribute. Internal PR is not just a means of allowing staff to heckle management, but to establish a systematic, two-way flow of information, for the benefit of everyone.
- Honesty – this really is the best policy when it comes to dealing with staff, as one fabrication or falsification will be remembered forever, and nothing you say afterwards will be regarded without some degree of suspicion. Honesty is your prime consideration when trying to decide what to say and how to say it.
- A match between external and internal messages. It can prove disheartening and certainly annoying if the image your employer creates is one which isn't replicated within the actual workplace – or that you cannot deliver promises that external campaigns are making on your behalf. Right from the start, ensure that internal and external messages are consistent, helping to improve the effectiveness of both internal and external strategies.
- Integration of the programme into the management process. Internal PR should not be an afterthought and a 'bonus' for staff, it should be integral to other management plans and programmes.

Planning the campaign

Assess your audience

If you want to plan an internal PR campaign, then as with any other activity, it's essential to fully understand your target audience before you begin.

Why not implement a staff communication audit – just as we considered when planning our media campaign (in fact, the two could be done at the same time). Such an exercise also makes a good start to the whole programme, demonstrating – by its very existence – the active intention of senior management to search for views and opinions. Of course, its ultimate success does then depend upon action being taken as a result!

A staff communications audit aims to understand and identify the differing needs and attitudes of various staff groups, looking at issues such as their perceived relationship with their employer or with management, and in particular looking at communications issues and the ways in which information is obtained and exchanged both with peers and those elsewhere up and down the management hierarchy. Obviously, the larger your staff base, the more relevant the exercise, as an interesting range of key concerns and issues will emerge from such an analysis, often challenging the set assumptions of your management team. Even though this seems to be an activity more appropriate for a large employee group, even the smallest number of staff – even a single employee – should respond positively to the task of identifying how internal communications could be improved.

When drafting the basic questionnaire, make sure you tailor the questions to meet the more specific needs of different staff groups. Sales reps, for example, will work in a very different manner from the general admin team and so questions have to reflect the ways in which people actually work. It may also be interesting to ask different staff groups how they assume other sections receive information – and check these perceptions against reality.

Identify appropriate activities

Your assessment of the communications mechanisms already in place – whether as a result of a full audit, or simply by summarizing the mechanisms you know already exist – will probably demonstrate that your underlying policy, whether overt or subconscious, has been based more on a day to day, 'need to know' approach. This is not necessarily due to management secrecy but more to avoid overloading staff with what you consider to be irrelevant information. However, if it's obvious that things could be improved, you need to identify those activities most appropriate to the nature of your employee base and use them more frequently and more effectively. It's also important to note that your staff will be gaining a lot of their information informally – in the canteen, as office gossip, the corridor meeting. Don't try to deny or squash these activities – in fact, if the quality of information is generally improved, then it could be that some of these informal mechanisms are just as effective as than some of the more formal.

Strategic activities

If you decide that you would benefit from a more structured approach to communications, consider the following activities and select those which will best suit the nature of your organization:

Internal publications

If you feel your organization is of a large enough size to merit the work involved, then a staff newsletter is a good vehicle for circulating general information, and it can even be mailed to wider audiences, including suppliers and distributors. The rapid development in computer-based printing technology has made the production of such newsletters cheap and easy, whilst relatively high production values can also be achieved. However, the main bone of contention is not usually one of design or production but one of content. It's easy for such a newsletter to be seen as a management mouthpiece so staff must be actively encouraged to contribute – but this is often easier said than done. One solution is to physically appoint a newsletter representative from each department or team within your organization, making them responsible for a round up of team news, and for the identification of those individuals who may be able to contribute something more interesting. Staff representatives must become part of any editorial meetings, or at least it must be easy for staff to contribute – even consider making the 'editor' of the newsletter someone from outside the senior management team.

Many of the guidelines for the production of 'market-facing' newsletters (see pages 71–8) also apply to internal publications, although content will be the main difference. When considering what to put into your internal newsletter, consider the following:

- Allocate a regular slot to each area of your organization which should be covered – do this by branding each section with its own sub-head, or less obviously by simply deciding the overarching editorial policy and setting it in stone.
- Make sure you also have a good balance between business and people news, and that the spread of people featured come from all parts of the organization, and from all levels.
- Try to avoid any editorial bias towards the more extrovert or able members of your organization – you'll probably find that they are the most willing to contribute, but the end result could appear unbalanced.
- Vary the tone of the pieces you include; for example, make sure 'light' pieces are featured as well as more thoughtful articles. Regular columns such as 'Day in the life' or 'My top ten', can focus upon anyone within your organization, from management to shop floor, adding interest for everyone.
- Provide opportunities for feedback in various ways – competitions, quizzes, even a letters page if you think that anyone will contibute!
- Also use the newsletter as a vehicle for any positive feedback received from clients or customers – it's often hard to find suitable methods of circulating this type of good news.

■ It's important to remember that staff newsletters, no matter how limited the circulation, will be in the public domain once published. They will be left around, passed on, taken home, so make sure that the content does not include anything unsuitable for external consumption – and this includes in-jokes and humorous articles, if they may cause offence when taken out of context.

■ The newsletter need not be printed if cost is an issue, but could be made available over the Internet or intranet – although this option is only appropriate if everyone within your organization has easy access to a computer terminal.

'Copying in'

You may have produced a brand new brochure, and are proudly displaying it in your reception area – but have you told all your staff about it? Copying staff in on external communications activities is important. Not only do they then feel valued rather than ignored, but they are also more aware of what the organization is up to within the marketplace, and can therefore speak with some knowledge if ever asked a question by a customer or client about any external activity that might be taking place.

Staff briefings

Most teams will have regular meetings which focus on work – but how often are meetings held which focus on news and information? It's probably not necessary to arrange a special meeting, but instead add a session to the agenda which gives you the opportunity to talk about more general issues, to find out what other members of the organization are up to and for your staff to raise queries or to ask about rumours currently circulating. A staff briefing is also a good way of disseminating important news which everyone must hear about at once. Many staff will welcome news presented in this way, as it will give them the opportunity to ask questions of those personnel most directly involved. It will also provide instant feedback from those groups most affected. If such briefings are organized on a regular basis – from once a week to once a year, depending on the scale of the exercise – then staff also know that they will soon have an opportunity to express their views on a certain topic and to invite comment from others. This results in the more efficient management of issues – a chance to gather them together in a receptive atmosphere, rather than receive them unprompted on a daily basis.

Notice boards

This may be the most prosaic vehicle but it's often the most effective, allowing fast, democratic dissemination of information. It may seem obvious, but physical noticeboards should be in a venue where all staff will have a chance to see them regularly, and out of date material must be removed promptly otherwise other information is instantly devalued. Intranet noticeboards or bulletin boards can also be effective, but can easily become cluttered if not edited assiduously, and also demand regular viewing. There is also the issue of who controls and edits the material published.

Videos and internet presentations

These are useful in situations where the same message has to be repeated frequently – when introducing a company to new recruits, for example, or if the same information has to be delivered in several locations simultaneously, such as a briefing prior to a product launch. However, both are expensive to produce, so for most organizations they will be a luxury if their sole purpose is to be used to inform staff. A multi-purpose presentation – one that can be used for any target audience, and containing messages which will remain current at least for the foreseeable future, is probably a more cost-effective, although less focused solution.

Entertaining

The value of entertaining staff – and the ways in which it can be done – has already been covered in Chapter 6 and it is an important element in a communications programme. Remember, however, that if you plan to use entertainment as an activity within your internal PR strategy then the aim is not necessarily to reward individuals for achieving specific targets but to thank them for their hard work, and demonstrate your commitment to their well-being, at whatever level and in whatever job. Try not to restrict yourself just to a Christmas 'do' – there are other times of the year when a social event could lift spirits, and there are also those corporate landmarks which could become a good excuse for a party!

Exercise

The Clean Sweeps are doing well – they've expanded rapidly, now have three separate offices operating in different local towns, and employ over 100 full- and part-time cleaning ladies. The management team knows that staff loyalty is vital and wants to use an internal PR campaign as one of the ways of encouraging this. What should they do?

PR Matrix

Unless you are a 'one-man-band', your staff will certainly be one of your target audiences. How do you plan to translate the messages aimed at this target audience into activities? Add these activities to your matrix.

8 | CRISIS MANAGEMENT

Almost daily it seems, one reads about one sort of disaster or another befalling an organization; perhaps one not too dissimilar to your own. Product recalls, redundancies, accidents, damage to reputation by association – there are a host of crises which, if they happened to you, could badly affect your organization, and if you are subsequently perceived as responding badly to the crisis, then the repercussions could be even worse. From the PR viewpoint, 'crisis management' is a structured approach to the handling of such events, aiming to put in place a communications strategy designed to direct the right information to the right people with maximum speed, minimizing the risk of misinformation and helping overall damage limitation.

Effective crisis management is based on advance planning. Of course you can never be sure what type of crisis may occur, or when it's going to happen, but there will certainly be a range of clearly identifiable scenarios (depending upon the nature of your organization and the way in which it operates) which could prompt a crisis. A crisis management plan starts with the active identification of such scenarios enabling you to then establish a range of communications mechanisms designed to manage immediate fallout, helping your staff concentrate on sorting out the core of the problem – the crisis itself. It's important to remember, right from the start, that crisis management is a management-driven communications strategy – although your PRO will advise and implement a lot of the required actions, management must be in control at all times.

Even if you cannot imagine your organization ever needing to plan in such a way, it may still be useful to read through the rest of this chapter. You may start to realize that you are not as invulnerable as you think, and that circumstances may change as your organization grows or develops, making a crisis seem less unlikely.

Developing a crisis management strategy

The following steps provide a basic action plan. This will result in a file of plans, papers and protocols which can be safely locked away, hopefully never to be used. Even so, they should be revisited regularly to make sure details are up to date. Once it is complete, you may want to consult your legal advisers, to double-check that anything you plan to do and say at a time of crisis won't get you into even more trouble!

Identify potential crises, and who would be affected by them

You will already be aware of the type of crises which could affect your organization, and probably have plans in place to deal with the practicalities of, say, shopfloor or production problems. Now we need to re-evaluate these crises from a communications point of view, and so planning should start with a structured analysis of *all* the possible problems that may face you at one time or another – without making yourself either too depressed or paranoid!

Here are a few of the more typical examples. As you'll see, some crises could be entirely your fault, but some will be out of your control, some will be easy to predict, others may hit you out of the blue. Horizon watching – the proactive monitoring of developing issues – plays an important role within this preliminary exercise, as it will help identify possible future threats, and review what's happening to other organizations similar to your own.

Consider:

Internal crises

- Are you a major local employer? Could redundancies have serious local repercussions?
- Is it likely that your workforce would ever come out on strike?

- What would happen if one of your products or services suddenly gave serious cause for concern? Might you ever have to instigate a major product recall?
- Do you handle or store products or materials that could be dangerous if stolen or misplaced?
- Do you issue an annual financial statement – what would be the impact if your results were worse than predicted?

External crises

- Are you associated with products, manufacturing processes or research techniques that could attract negative publicity, for whatever reason?
- What would be the effect of fire, flood or other serious damage to your property?
- Would you suffer if a crisis happened to one of your major customers or suppliers?
- Are there any issues bubbling under at the moment – results of externally commissioned reports or government committees for example – that could have a damaging effect upon your organization if the resulting conclusions went against you or your line of business?
- Is there an organization similar to your own which is currently attracting bad publicity? Could you be tarnished with the same brush if the climate of opinion rapidly changes?

The role of the web in crisis development

The web is proving to be an unwelcome catalyst in the manufacture of crises. Bad publicity which may have only a transient presence in a national daily newspaper can hang around on a web site for weeks, months or even years with the power to reach thousands of individuals on a daily basis. And the growing prevalence of 'suck sites', actively targeting particular organizations, can prove a particularly irritating thorn in the side for those unlucky to attract such dedicated attention. Such sites can also be linked to thousands of other related sites, providing a constant reference point for innocent visitors. If you think that you may be at risk from a web-induced crisis, then companies do exist which can constantly monitor the web on your behalf – although vital for large corporations, you may not need such a comprehensive service but, whatever your size, regular monitoring of selected sites will do no harm.

Preparation activities

Once you've identified the possible crises, then list the audiences that would be affected – customers, clients, staff, shareholders, suppliers etc. The effect on each needs to be considered, an appropriate response drafted and the most suitable mechanism identified – and we'll look at a range of specific crisis-management mechanisms in this chapter. The media will play a crucial role in the management of this response phase – at best helping broadcast the information you want to disseminate, at worst provoking or exacerbating a crisis by spreading information which is either untrue, or which was not destined for public consumption in an unedited form.

It's impossible to be too specific about what to do – every industry is different, and every organization within it will be faced with a different set of challenges. But the following ideas provide a basic approach to the construction of a crisis management plan, and will at least start you thinking along the most appropriate lines. First, let's consider what you can do to prepare your organization for the worst:

A cascade communications plan

In the case of an emergency, or if the media are banging on your door, then your most senior staff must be available to represent the company – they will have both the authority to answer questions effectively, and the confidence to manage what could be a very stressful experience. Fielding an untrained, panicking office manager – and it has happened – will only end up sending a host of negative messages to all your target audiences, further compounding the potentially bad publicity brewing as a result of the developing crisis.

But time is of the essence – if a crisis breaks in the middle of the night, or during a quiet time of year, senior staff may not always be immediately available, or on site, when a situation develops. In order to prepare for such an eventuality, create a list of all those who are authorized to speak on behalf of the company in the event of a crisis: the MD or CEO; directors; senior managers; and any other senior staff who are on site most of the time – this may include finance directors for example, or HR managers. Don't forget your to include your PRO in the list, as well as any senior consultants you may have working for you – you may even want to include other trusted advisers, such as lawyers or accountants, if you can be confident in their response. Remember that most of the contacts will simply be required to field immediate questions in an intelligent, calm manner, whilst waiting for senior management to become available. For each name list work, mobile and home phone numbers, email and fax, to ensure contact can be made 24 hours a day.

Then create a cascade communications plan, which will enable – if necessary – any individual within your organization to alert the most senior member of staff available. Indicate who should be called first – a line manager or the PRO for example – enabling them to make the decision as to who to contact next, but allow anyone within the organization to initiate the chain. This will make sure you are not left 'speechless' at a time of major panic.

Crisis briefing

Obviously, everyone on your cascade list needs to understand what would be expected of them if they were contacted as a crisis was unfolding. Hold a briefing session, to inform everyone of their roles and responsibilities and put systems in place to ensure that everyone is rebriefed (by memo or other appropriate means) of any changes that subsequently take place. New recruits must also be included in the loop at whatever level is appropriate, and so your personnel team needs to be involved in order to ensure that the right amount of information is given to each new appointee.

Prepare 'holding statements'

Once you've identified and documented those who can talk on your behalf, then decide what they can say. Unless there are already fully apprised of the crisis, you run the risk of leaving them flapping in ignorance, able only to say 'no comment' – the worst response of all!

If an unexpected crisis hits your organization, it's often the case that no one knows what is going on for a significant time, but during this time you may well start to receive urgent calls from a variety of sources, not least the media, all wanting to know what's happening. If you can prepare 'holding statements' in advance – ideally using information drawn from your existing, practical contingency plans – then they can be issued immediately by anyone within your organization authorized to do so. Once again, holding statements will be highly specific to the nature of the crisis you are attempting to contain, but make sure the statement indicates that you are aware of the problem, that you regret any damage or distress that it has caused (if relevant), that you are currently doing something about it and that you will issue a fuller statement at a later time – and if you can indicate an exact time and place then even better. Holding statements must also be available via your home page (see below for more on the role of the web). If you were already well aware that a crisis was about to strike (you have just announced a major round of redundancies, for example) then you will be able to prepare such statements with greater confidence and accuracy, and can already have arrangements in hand for a full briefing session later that same day.

If a crisis does happen, then your most senior staff must be kept free in order to address enquiries from the press or from your most important clients or other contacts (as well as deal with the crisis itself), but you may also find that your switchboard quickly becomes jammed with calls from a wide range of other individuals, all demanding more information. Therefore, entrust a holding statement to the most senior member of your reception team, who can use it to respond immediately to any customer, client or staff enquiries.

Once drafted, these statements must be kept somewhere secure but easily accessible by the right personnel. Under no circumstances must they be issued accidentally, to the press or to anyone else, (thus precipitating a crisis that never would have happened otherwise) or be used by staff members unauthorized to do so.

'Question and Answer' documents

If you can prepare a list of answers to the most likely questions then this will also prove invaluable, and will immediately provide a focused response to immediate queries, and possibly deflect more aggressive questioning at least for a short time. Sketch a draft document for each of your potential crisis scenarios, to provide answers to hypothetical questions – you may also find this exercise useful in making you think more broadly about the possible implications of a crisis situation, and the ways you would deal with it.

Prepare a crisis media liaison strategy

The media will play a vital role in the ongoing development of a crisis, for good or otherwise and whether you want them to or not: the media can even cause a crisis, so it helps if you can encourage them to be your ally right from the start.

Once again, it greatly depends on the exact nature of the crisis as to what you do, but you can certainly start to prepare the ground. For example:

Crisis press contact list

Just as you prepared a cascade contact list for your staff, prepare a list of the most important journalists to contact straight away. Given the fact that most crises are of immediate news interest, your list will probably comprise mainly local or national journalists in print and broadcast media, freelancers, special correspondents and the newsdesks of relevant publications or news services. Your trade press will also want to know more: add weekly publications to the immediate circulation list, and although monthly publications may seem less relevant in the heat of the moment, don't forget to inform them in due course.

As we have said before, trying to create closer links with local journalists (in particular) can reap benefits during a time of crisis, especially if they have had a chance to get to know your organization and some of the personalities working for it – as a result, they are more likely to be 'on your side' if a serious crisis occurs.

Draft skeleton press releases

Once again, drawing on your list of predicted crises, draft a series of press releases which could be issued as soon as possible after the crisis breaks – as soon as you have something positive or informative to say that is. The press will want to know more, and will need authorized comprehensive information. Once drafted, again, keep in a secure location, accessible only by your PRO and by senior staff members authorized to approve its issue – it is imperative that such releases should never be issued in error.

Prepare a 'Company profile'

General information about your organization can prove invaluable in a host of situations, especially crises. If you are suddenly faced with a barrage of requests for more background details, then having a ready-made, fully approved 'company profile' could be the answer to your prayers. In Chapter 4 we looked in detail at how to prepare such a profile.

Media training

As a crisis develops, then your senior staff may suddenly find themselves pushed into the media spotlight, and so it's important that they know at least the fundamentals of how to act in such a situation, in order to give them confidence and to ensure their performance is a credit to your organization. We looked at media training briefly in Chapter 3, but if you feel that your organization could be prone to problem situations, then it may be worth investing in training geared specifically to handling crises. During such training sessions, senior staff will experience the type of media attention that a crisis might generate, and will be able to develop the proactive skills required to deal with the media in high pressure situations. They will also be able to physically experience the feeling of a telephone or TV interview – invaluable for anyone who has never come face to face with a journalist before. Such training can be expensive, but the knowledge gained by a few key individuals can also be filtered down to other senior team members.

Informing staff

Staff at every level must be aware of your crisis management plans, in order to make sure that they assist your management team, and certainly do not talk to the media on behalf of your organization. Look at your internal PR mechanisms (see Chapter 7), and use those to help inform your staff of the plans you are putting in place, especially those elements which may require their active participation, such as the cascade communications plan. You may feel a more formal approach is necessary in order to underline the importance of abiding by the rules you have established. A dedicated leaflet, issued to each staff member on joining the company, may provide a practical solution – but make sure it is updated as regularly as every other part of your overall plan.

Web sites and dark sites

In time of crisis your web site will be a main point of contact for many of your target audiences who want to access up-to-date information as quickly as possible. It's therefore vital that your web site responds immediately, in some form or other, to events as they unfold. Depending upon the scale of the crisis, it may be relatively easy to quickly add some new information to your home page, in order to provide an immediate summary of the situation, and an indication of when more information will follow. Some larger organizations create 'dark sites' – fully engineered web sites which only go online if a crisis occurs, replacing the existing home page within half an hour of the alarm being sounded. Although initially capable of carrying only the briefest of information the site also carries the corporate profile, and then becomes a repository for all the crisis related information as it comes on stream. Its mere presence will indicate that an organization is taking the crisis very seriously.

Dark sites are expensive (think how much it cost to create your everyday web site) and so although really the preserve of the major corporation, a smaller scale version could be considered, or a pop-up screen which could launch automatically as soon as the home page starts to load. If you decide to create a dark site, make sure it's stored on CD or ZIP Disk so that a copy can be taken directly to an ISP should you be unable to run the program yourself – due to fire or other major disaster.

Rehearse

Once you have your plans in place, then a 'dress rehearsal' may be worth considering, especially if your strategy depends upon a number of staff, possibly in different locations, each with a different role to play. Such an exercise can also show exactly where weak links exist, and which staff still feel under-prepared. If you employ an outside PR agency then use them to help you, as staff often find it easier to 'pretend' or role play with an independent adviser acting as a facilitator, rather than amongst themselves. Once again, specialist agencies exist which can provide specific training in handling crises.

Reviewing crisis management plans

It's crucial that the plans you have so carefully drawn up remain current and valid. Make sure that whoever is responsible for them reviews them regularly, and that specific triggers are identified which justify an immediate review – staff changes, for example, or changes to product details. Any revisions must be circulated immediately to those who need to know, and the information reiterated within any communication which forms part of the overall strategy.

Implementation

Despite the care you take over your plan, you will, hopefully, never have to use it – although you will find that certain elements (the corporate profile or media training for example) will prove highly useful in other aspects of your work.

If the worst comes to the worst, however, you'll need to put your plan into action. Specific actions will depend entirely on the nature of the crisis facing you, but here's a general summary of what to do:

- Implement the cascade communications mechanism as quickly as possible – alert all senior staff and make sure they are available in person or on the phone.
- If your building has been damaged or destroyed quickly identify an alternative location as your PR office for the immediate period – this could be the office of your PR consultancy, a sympathetic local business, or even your own home.
- Don't panic – whilst assessing the scale of the crisis instruct your PRO to:
  - refine the holding statements with the most immediate information – issue to all authorized members of staff and release via the web site; trigger your dark site or pop-up windows; revise all other paperwork you have already prepared;
  - give a deadline by which more information will be available;
  - if necessary make arrangements for the delivery of a press statement – this can be given at the front door of your building, within a suitable meeting room or (if your building has been rendered unusable) wherever is most practical;
  - as soon as you can, revise your press release and issue it to your press list by fax or email; include the revised Q&A sheet and corporate profile.

As the crisis progresses and hopefully is controlled, issue further regular statements using all the channels identified in order to keep your audiences up to date. Monitor ongoing press coverage, especially if you sense the tide is turning against you – if so, move quickly to reassure all your target audiences using whatever evidence you can.

Exercise

You own a firework factory, situated next to a river, employing over 100 local people. The bottom has fallen out of the firework market and the future looks gloomy – in addition, one of your favourite firework ingredients has recently been labelled highly toxic by the European Firework Council and banned from use, even though you still have over 20 barrels of the chemical sitting in a shed in your yard.

What possible crises face you? How should you prepare?

PR Matrix

Crisis management falls outside the remit of ongoing PR as hopefully you will never need to use it. However, if you think that adopting some of the strategies outlined here might be beneficial – or that a full plan may even be necessary – add this to your objectives and set aside a separate strategy development programme for crisis management planning.

9 | **SPECIALIST PR**

Most PR programmes operate within fairly modest parameters – target audiences are easy to identify, objectives are clear, and implementation focuses on a range of tried and tested activities. But every now and again you may find yourself needing more specialist advice. This chapter looks at two such PR 'disciplines' – Government Affairs, and Financial PR – in order to give an overview, and to provide some guidelines on what to do if you need specialist help.

Government Affairs or lobbying

If your list of target audiences includes any elected official, at either local or national level, then you could find yourself embarking upon a programme of 'Government Affairs' or lobbying. Your main aim is to inform elected representatives of the needs of your organization or your industry, in order to help direct the development of those local or national policies which affect your organization. In business, Government Affairs campaigns usually fall under the 'Corporate PR' banner, and run in parallel with consumer or trade PR campaigns, taking either a leading or background role as the need arises. For any organization promoting or fighting a particular issue or cause, Government Affairs is often the lynchpin of the PR strategy.

Even the smallest organization may find itself launching a Government Affairs campaign, albeit a modest one, as a result of one of three main drivers:

To support a trade-driven initiative

All industries have 'issues' – regulatory, legal, legislative – which affect the way an individual business operates. Such issues are discussed and debated at industry-level, but are also raised with Government representatives, mainly through dialogue between the Government and trade bodies, specialist advisers, and leading organizations within the industry concerned. If a smaller organization wants to become more actively involved, perhaps for specific business reasons or as a way of raising profile, a Government Affairs campaign can provide an effective vehicle, allowing an organization to more effectively join the larger debate whilst lobbying for its own particular cause.

To support or raise awareness of a broader issue

For non-commercial organizations, a Government Affairs programme is often essential to the success of an issue-based campaign, and can generate high profile PR opportunities.

Commercial organizations that feel particularly strongly about certain non-business issues sometimes choose to lead the argument from the front and lobby proactively for change. Although the issue chosen will be relevant to their industry, it may also reflect a broader set of values with which an organization wishes to be associated. Championing a 'good cause' may therefore become a PR activity in its own right, and can prove an ideal vehicle for a host of promotional activities, raising profile and enhancing reputation along the way. Supporting a 'non-business' issue does have inherent risks, however – you may find yourself spending more and more money on an activity which is only loosely related to your business goals, and if the issue becomes even slightly controversial you can run the risk of alienating a section of your target audiences, even the Government.

In response to an unforeseen development

The worst-case scenario – to suddenly find that your organization is likely to be at the receiving end of some damaging legislation, or to discover that an issue has suddenly arisen which could prove a serious threat to your livelihood. Under these circumstances, a campaign can be launched with some degree of panic, and lack coherence of both message and effort, vital if it is to achieve both short and long-term objectives – however, in reality, most campaigns *are* launched in just these circumstances and still achieve valuable results, so don't be too disheartened if you start your campaign feeling hurried or rushed.

Implementing a Government Affairs campaign

Government Affairs programmes can prove costly, time-consuming and – if the tide of opinion turns against you – potentially damaging, so make sure you use this particular PR tool for good reasons, anchored firmly to your overriding aims and objectives. You may find that you can add little to the work already being done by your trade association, or by a larger, related organization, and so all you need to do is monitor the situation and find opportunities to add support when appropriate.

But if you work within an industry which is continuously beset by issues and debates, a more proactive approach could reap valuable rewards, minimizing potentially damaging developments and raising your profile within target groups as a champion of just causes. Capitalize on any 'horizon watching' activities – proactive monitoring of emerging industry developments – that your PR or sales team undertakes, and identify those issues needing more investigation, so that you are prepared in advance should an issue blow up quickly, or are in a good position to launch a campaign if the climate of opinion is in your favour. At the very least, you can put together a skeleton campaign plan which can be implemented should a serious crisis occur – see Chapter 8 on Crisis Management for more information.

If you have decided to launch a Government Affairs campaign, here are a few golden rules:

- Lobbying is not a restricted practice so if you decide to add lobbying to your list of PR activities, don't assume that you will automatically need the assistance of a specialist consultancy. In fact, Government Affairs consultancies should not actively lobby at all – this should be left to the individual or organization concerned.

- If you are responding to an emerging issue, then you must act as quickly as possible, both to try and effect damage limitation and to start what can be a long process as soon as you can. The quicker off the mark the better the results.

- Always start by going to your local MP – not only does this help build bridges with a highly influential member of your local community, but it also serves to hasten the general political process. The best way to begin is by preparing a written outline summarizing the issue or problem as you perceive it, together with your suggested solution. Send this to your MP asking them to act upon it and to forward your letter to the appropriate department. Your MP should then send on your correspondence with a covering letter – this serves to fast-track your concern, greatly improving the chances of notice being taken. Capitalize upon the contact you have made with your MP by keeping them informed of both the progress of your campaign, and of the development of your business in general.

- As well as your MP, contact your industry trade body or even a local business association such as the Chamber of Commerce, asking them to support you in your fight. Once again, a letter to a Minister will carry more weight if delivered under the banner of a trade organization. Trade bodies are also used to working within the political environment and so will be able to provide good advice on how to achieve your goals.

- Civil servants must also be approached – many issues revolve around technicalities and detail rather than the broad brush of Government policy, and so a necessary activity is to arrange a meeting between an expert from within your organization and the relevant Government official dealing with the relevant portfolio (the Government department will be able to give you this information). If the issue is current, then civil servants are often very happy to gain a better under-standing of the implications of proposed legislation.

- As we have already noted, it isn't necessary to use a specialist consultancy, but if a bad decision could prompt a crisis, then hiring such an agency might be worth considering: this is particularly true if the issue facing you has come out of the blue. Professional consultancies should not lobby for you – this role must be left with the senior members of your management team, and to a certain extent to your PRO if he or she is sufficiently experienced. Use your consultant to guide you through all the necessary stages and procedures, to identify the specific levels within Government which you need to influence, and to make you aware of the political nuances which will be in play. This is where they will earn their money, and you must take full advantage of their skills if you choose to use them.

■ Government Affairs consultancies are rarely 'unethical' these days – if they were they would soon get an unsavoury reputation and go out of business pretty quickly. There is currently some debate within the industry as to whether a 'code of practice' should become mandatory for all agencies offering Government Affairs consultancy, in order to avoid misuse of access or influence. But if lobbying is already the right of every individual then some form of discriminatory code could imply that every non-registered agency is somehow less able or less 'ethical' than others – and as a result could be seen to be favouring certain agencies over others. Whatever the issues involved, if you do need to use a consultancy, then check their references pretty thoroughly, and make sure their experience has been gained in cases similar to your own.

■ If, as part of your lobbying activities, you need to gain the support of audiences outside the Government circle, then you need to supplement your Government Affairs programme with a range of associated PR activities. Tailor some of your ongoing PR to match lobbying objectives – try to place some discursive or controversial articles within your trade press, for example, in which you can state your arguments and declare your support for a particular cause. Host a seminar which focuses on the issue, or sponsor a relevant event. Web sites are a highly useful vehicle for issue-based PR, as they can be used to state arguments clearly and concisely, can supply additional detail at any level required, and can provide up-to-date progress reports.

However, when integrating your Government Affairs campaign with ongoing PR work, make sure that you continue to work towards *all* your stated objectives – you don't want to bore audiences by always going on about the same issue, or becoming associated solely with a particular campaign, affecting overall audience perception.

Financial PR

Financial PR specialists talk to two main audiences, the financial press and city analysts, and focus on two main types of activity, investor relations and City press relations. Companies can choose to appoint an in-house specialist, or use consultancy. Most large plcs use both.

As with most forms of PR, the overriding principle of financial communications is that ongoing relationships and a mutual understanding between a business and its key audiences should ensure that its case is both well understood and sympathetically received when it has something important to say.

Companies would certainly be well advised to call upon Financial PR specialists if they are considering a listing on the Stock Exchange within the foreseeable future. Although not a mandatory requirement, any company wanting to float will have to issue a variety of press releases and other informative documents and there are strict procedures which govern the way such material is written and distributed, with serious penalties for any transgression. Consultancies, with their extensive experience of the transaction process, can make sure their clients keep to the right side of the law, whilst also honouring obligations and commitments. The vast majority of organizations feel, therefore, that the assistance of a specialist consultancy is invaluable, and is one less thing to worry about at what can be a highly stressful time.

Finding a consultant

Finding a suitable consultancy is not difficult; your financial advisers will provide a number of recommendations, selecting agencies with a good track record and with specific experience either in your market sector or of handling companies similar to your own.

As you start your selection process you may find that a recommended consultancy is already working for a direct competitor – but whereas this would be a serious concern if you were planning a consumer or trade PR campaign, within the more rarefied world of financial PR this is less of a worry. Financial consultancies are limited in number, and if a consultancy specializes in a certain industry sector, then it will invariably be working for organizations similar to your own. Timing will be the issue, rather than a conflict of professional loyalties – if a direct competitor is planning to float at around the same time as your organization, then don't share consultancies.

One of the most important selection criteria is that the client consultant relationship is a good one – even if you feel that you have no way of judging whether one consultancy is better than another, gut instinct and personal chemistry will help you decide. You are about to embark upon a very intensive period of co-operative endeavour and so it's vital that you get on well with the personalities involved.

Financial PR campaigns

Your financial consultant will personally brief city analysts on the nature of your organization, using information prepared in consultation with you. Such meetings are heavily regulated by the Stock Exchange to ensure that information is released in an orderly way so that no unfair advantage can be gained by any one individual. The consultant will aim to generate an 'exit survey' as a result of these meetings, in order to give you some indication of the feeling within the City about your forthcoming flotation.

Financial PR consultancies are in daily contact with the financial press, who are becoming increasingly important and influential in the City. In terms of press work, the objective is to feed quality stories to key financial journalists, and also to those journalists interested in your particular industry sector. Your consultant will be constantly looking for stories, especially relating to your company accounts, which will be of particular interest to potential investors. As well as financial information, such as business results, stories which can demonstrate industry trends will also be placed, to help give a fuller picture of your organization, its status within your industry, and of the value it represents.

Your relationship with a financial PR consultancy is often short-term and highly intensive, but many consultancies are retained by their clients following a flotation, and are brought in to handle major financial announcements or other relevant issues. They can also play an important role in Corporate PR strategies, bringing a City perspective to the development and implementation of any longer term programmes.

Exercise

As you'll have gathered, you'll only ever need this type of specialist PR if a very specific set of circumstances arises, or if you are actively involved in the championing of specific causes, so a dedicated exercise is less relevant.

However, if either scenario is part of your overall business objectives, then lobbying or financial PR may need to be considered and added to your Matrix.

10 USING PR PROFESSIONALS – IN-HOUSE AND EXTERNAL

If your PR campaign is proving so successful that your resources are starting to buckle under the strain, or you know already that you'll need specialist advice in order to run your ideal programme, then you have to consider hiring professional help. Your main options are to employ an in-house PR officer, pitching the appointment to suit the level of expertise you require, or to hire an external consultant. In this chapter we look at each of these options in more detail.

What type of PR help do you need?

PR help comes in three main forms:

PR Consultancies

Operating as independent agencies, sometimes as part of a national or international group, consultancies offer dedicated PR expertise, often within a particular industry sector or discipline. Consultancies can bring the advantages of manpower and specialist knowledge available as and when you need it. Using a consultancy can be expensive – their average annual fee may equal the salaries of two in-house professionals – and so this option is probably only worth considering if your campaign requires a significant input of time either for a limited period (a launch phase for example), or you want to implement a wide ranging PR campaign and sustain this over the longer term. Administration and management of the 'client/consultant relationship' can represent a significant part of consultancy start up costs, and so the longer you maintain the relationship the more productive the outcome will be.

Consultancies can deliver significant manpower, both in the day-to-day running of your PR programme, and if a major event demands a number of extra, experienced hands. A consultancy will also handle all programme administration which, as we've already seen, can prove very time consuming and laborious. But one of the most important advantages is that a consultancy has the time to think proactively on your behalf, and to apply its creative skills to your PR campaign. It also has access to and knowledge of a wide range of PR resources, such as media databases, press contacts, training providers, event organizers, and other more specialist advisers in other branches of PR.

Every client on a consultancy's books is termed an 'account' and, depending upon the amount of work involved, a team of PR professionals will be assigned to each account, to ensure that there is always someone fully briefed on your PR programme and able to provide answers to immediate queries. Account teams often comprise an Account Director, who manages the PR programme, and an Account Executive, who handles day-to-day administration, and they in turn will be supported by secretarial or other administrative assistance. Additional levels of seniority also exist, but it depends upon the size of the Consultancy as to the nature of the hierarchy in place.

One common criticism of consultancies is that clients often seem to spend most of their time speaking to the account executive, the most junior member of the team, than with the director who persuaded them to hire the consultancy in the first place – there is also the problem of team changes as consultancy staff change jobs or move on, taking their accumulated expertise with them.

The reverse is equally true – consultants find it difficult to run a programme when they only have access to junior management, having worked primarily with senior staff during the programme development phase. If only junior management remains closely involved then important, strategic decisions cannot be taken, top-level approval can be delayed, and if the decision-making skill of a junior manager is doubted by a senior consultant (as can often happen) then the whole relationship can be undermined. The overriding aim of a PR programme is to communicate the essence of your organization, and it's therefore vital that senior staff remain closely involved in the ways in which this communication is managed and implemented.

'Full service' marketing agencies also often offer PR, but rarely can they provide the fully resourced service of a dedicated PR agency, instead usually offering the skills of an individual PR practitioner. If you only require limited input, then PR provided in this way can prove more cost-effective than using a consultancy, and the resulting campaign should integrate fully with other marketing activities, if the agency is handling these for you as well.

Retainer agreements

Most consultancies want to establish a 'retainer' agreement, a regular commitment from each client to use the agency for so many hours per month, or for a set fee, based on the scope and nature of the campaign. If you go ahead with such an arrangement, then you are committed to paying this amount every month, plus additional expenses and other costs depending upon the nature of the activities undertaken. This enables you to budget for PR with more accuracy, but also represents a financial commitment, which you must make sure you make the most of.

Managing a consultancy

Don't think that hiring a consultancy will relieve you from all PR responsibilities – the relationship needs to be managed, and depends quite heavily upon the involvement of your senior staff in order to approve actions, take strategic decisions and act as spokespeople for your organization (and we'll look at these responsibilities in more detail later in this chapter). It's not uncommon for consultancies to be under-used, simply because their client can't find time to provide sufficient input to keep the programme running. A good consultancy should flag such problems fairly readily, but it is important to be aware of the commitment you will need to make to the relationship before you embark upon it.

Conversely, you may overuse your agency, particularly during the first few months of your campaign activities – most consultancies tend to take the longer view during this period, and assume that the workload will even out, but they will also point out if this overwork is consistent and either suggest a period of 'rest' so that the balance is restored, or that you increase your budget and hire more of their time.

Independent consultants

Many PR professionals turn freelance and can offer advice or input at a variety of levels. Many specialise in a particular field (often based on their personal career experience), whilst others offer an all-round capability.

An independent professional is usually more cost-effective for a smaller organization, although as they can only offer their time and expertise they will not be able to provide either continuous availability or access to the resources that consultancies offer. Once again, depending upon the nature of the assistance you require, freelancers can be hired project by project, or you can decide upon a longer-term relationship, including them within your strategy and relying upon their input over a sustained period of time. Freelance consultants often become regarded as part of a marketing team, and gain a thorough understanding of the dynamics of an organization and the market sector in which it operates. As a result such a relationship can run for many years – and I can speak from personal experience!

On the other hand (and loath though I am to say it) a consultant working alone can often find it difficult to generate new ideas year after year, simply because they have worked so closely with their client for a long period of time, and because they can't bounce ideas off other members of a team. For these reasons it might be useful to employ an agency from time to time, simply to breathe new life into an ongoing campaign.

In-house PRO

Deciding whether or not you need to employ an in-house PRO depends greatly on the scope of your PR campaign – the level of expertise which you think you require, and the amount of administrative support needed, both to run the programme of activities and manage the feedback it prompts. The cost of hiring an agency compared to a new member of staff makes the employment of a dedicated PRO suddenly seem very attractive, especially if you know that PR will play an integral role in your ongoing marketing.

It's worth remembering that your in-house PRO need not be a senior member of the team. As we've already seen, a lot of PR requires basic administrative and project management skills, and it's often these which are in shortest supply. Appointing the equivalent of an Account Executive, for example, will give you someone with a good combination of basic PR understanding and administrative experience. PRO's can also play very senior roles within organizations – even at board level.

Another alternative is to employ your PRO either as a part-timer, or with PR as only a part of their overall responsibility. Although this is often the most common option especially when using PR for the first time, it does have serious drawbacks. PR *must* be proactive as well as reactive – time needs to be spent identifying possible new PR angles or opportunities, and if your PRO's other responsibilities become too demanding then this valuable thinking and planning time soon drops to the bottom of the agenda, or is forgotten completely.

Combining talents to form a PR team

Of course, you don't have to choose exclusively between the options listed above. A combination may provide a successful and possibly more cost-effective solution, enabling you to avoid committing too many resources in one direction.

For example, employing a junior in-house PRO with a senior level freelance consultant could result in good management of strategic direction with adequate administrative support. The junior could benefit from the consultant's expertise, whilst the company would only hire the senior freelance when needed. The reverse of this arrangement could also prove valuable – senior skills brought in house, with lower level admin bought as needed.

Consultancies can be hired on a project-by-project basis if required, which may prove more cost-effective than embarking on a long-term relationship, although in-house support will be required in order to manage the relationship. Bringing consultancies – or consultants for that matter – in on short-term projects also gives you the chance to assess how good they really are before considering offering them a longer-term contract.

Finding help

It's all very well deciding that you need PR help, but trying to find the ideal PR partner can be a rather laborious business. Let's look again at the three main categories and see how the process works.

Finding a consultancy

PR agencies can be found all over the country – a quick look at your local trade directory will soon show just how many there are in your local area, never mind the more specialist agencies which may be further afield. It certainly isn't the case that you have to go to a major city to find the best consultancies (unless you require more specialist advice, of the kind we covered in Chapter 9), but even local options may prove confusingly broad. Here are some useful starting points to help you in your search:

Professional bodies and advisers

The UK PR industry boasts two main professional associations, the IPR (the Institute of Public Relations) and the PRCA (the Public Relations Consultancy Association). Both run 'matchmaking' services, providing lists of member agencies which meet basic selection criteria, but it must be remembered that the results will necessarily be selective as not all consultancies are members of either organization.

If you are hunting for a more specialist agency, then your own industry trade body may be able to advise on the best-known consultancies in the field. For local advice, ask business advisers – accountants, bank managers, management consultants etc. – they often know the best local service companies around. If you are already using another marketing service such as a designer, copywriter or marketing agency, then they will also be able to help you. PR is often part of a marcomms remit, and such agencies often recommend their clients to buy in this more specialized service as and when it's required, unless, of course, they supply it themselves.

Reference sources

As mentioned above, many organizations have found trade directories and other business reference sources as good a way as any to start their search, especially if they particularly want a locally based agency. A search on the Internet will also provide some good leads, with the added advantage of corporate background in order to help you refine your search further. The trade press of the PR industry might also prove useful. As with many other marketing and business titles, PR publications are often available on the newsstand – and many agencies advertise within their pages or are featured in news reports, but by and large these tend to be either based in the cities or are larger consultancies.

Word of mouth

Most service companies know that recommendation is one of the best ways of generating new business, and PR consultancies are no exception. Ask around in your own local business community and find out who is using who. Those local marketing seminars, business events (such as those run by the Chamber of Commerce) or other gatherings and networking opportunities (so highly recommended by PR professionals!) are also another good opportunity to gather for opinion and advice. And of course, if your local PR consultancies are worth their salt, you should already know about them through their own PR campaigns!

Hiring a consultancy

As your list of likely consultancies starts to grow, you need to start applying a few selection criteria in order to help filter the options. Consider:

Location

Would a local agency be more suitable, perhaps because your target audiences are primarily local, and knowledge of the local business community would be an advantage? There is also the added benefit of proximity – you can visit your advisers easily, and they are on the spot should an urgent issue arise.

Speciality

Would you prefer a consultancy that already works for related companies within your particular industry? Using such an agency can reap valuable benefits: they'll already be very familiar with your target media, and have a thorough understanding of the drivers affecting your industry. You may even find that you can take advantage of economies of scale, if your PRO can attend a trade fair on behalf of a number of related clients, then your particular share of the cost can be reduced. However, you do need to be careful of conflicts of interest – make sure that the consultancy isn't already working for a competitor organization, although it should advise you of any problems it can foresee. Often agencies working in a very close-knit industry sector create 'Chinese walls' between account teams (organizational barriers to make sure no information is exchanged, accidentally or otherwise). This enables two competing clients to be serviced effectively, but if you feel uneasy about such an arrangement then continue to shop around. Specialist agencies are not always on your doorstep – as often as not they will be based in a city and charge fees accordingly, so you may have to balance higher cost and reduced access against the advantage of specialist knowledge.

Size and resources

As soon as you start to research PR agencies, you'll soon find out that some are very small and some employ hundreds of staff in locations around the world. For some clients, size and resource is important, and the knowledge that they can take advantage of an international presence is invaluable especially if they are launching an international campaign. If you are planning only a modest campaign – and only a modest spend – then you may feel that your small account would be lost in the corridors of such an agency, and perhaps feel that a smaller consultancy would suit both you and your organization better.

Experience

Perhaps one of the most reassuring criteria is the knowledge that a consultancy has worked on similar accounts in the past, even if it brands itself as a general consultancy. Experience of working with organizations similar to your own brings an immediate appreciation of the internal and external dynamics at play. The agency may even be working with complementary organizations, which will ensure current knowledge of the relevant media, therefore increasing the effectiveness of your PR campaign.

Professional standards

As in any industry, PR consultancies are increasingly feeling the need to demonstrate proven accreditation for their working methods, primarily by achieving international quality standards. If a consultancy can demonstrate achievements at this level, then this is undoubtedly impressive and an indication of the serious approach they take towards their business – but as such accreditation can cost a lot of money, don't be put off if a much smaller consultancy does not boast such official endorsement. A recommendation from a satisfied client may provide just as much reassurance.

Setting up a pitch

When an organization decides that they need consultancy help, they often invite two or three agencies to present their ideas at what is known as a competitive pitch, or 'beauty parade'. You should only really consider this route if your PR budget is of a reasonable size, or your campaign requires a reasonable amount of input. From the consultancy's point of view the competitive pitch, though an essential part of the PR business, is time-consuming, expensive and uncertain, and will only be considered if worth the possible outcome. You don't want to earn a reputation for wasting time.

In practice, many organizations invite both specialist and general agencies to pitch against each other, in order to weigh up whether a local agency could deliver as good a service as a remotely located specialist consultancy. If you have decided that a pitch is the best way to go forward then the following guidelines may prove helpful:

Initial contact

Once you have drawn up a shortlist of suitable consultancies, arrange an initial meeting, and visit their offices in order to gain some initial impressions. Your aim is to find out more about the agency, and confirm in your own mind that they could work effectively for you. Of course you need to provide a very basic summary of your needs – if nothing else, you need to eliminate the risk of a conflict of interest – but save a fuller brief for later: the desired outcome at this point is a mutual interest in going further.

Briefing

Write formally to all the agencies you have selected inviting them to pitch for the business. Indicate when the pitch will take place. If you can, set a date there and then, and ask the agency team to make an appointment for a formal briefing.

In order to create a level playing field, and to help your final assessment, try to make sure that the briefing you give each consultancy is essentially the same – the way the briefing meeting progresses once an agency starts to ask questions is, however, another matter. In fact, the way they respond to a brief – the questions asked, the issues raised etc. – often gives you a good idea of the way they will handle your campaign.

Make your brief as comprehensive as possible. Gather together company literature in order to provide background information, and to give a flavour of the image your organization currently projects. Provide a summary of your current marketing activities to indicate the context in which the PR plan will operate; the fundamental reasons why you've decided to use PR, or why you have decided to use an agency; your perception (or knowledge) of competitor activities and how successful or otherwise they've been. And last but not least, provide an outline – as you see it – of the aims and objectives of your PR campaign. Most agencies will refine this further to enable them to draw up a full strategy.

Budget

The issue of budget is a tricky one – on one hand, you may have an idea of exactly what you want to achieve, but need to know how much a consultancy will charge; on the other hand, you may have a fixed budget in mind and would rather see what an agency can do within those budgetary constraints. If your budget is relatively fixed, then the latter approach is probably the fairer one, and it often forces a consultancy to be more creative.

The proposal and presentation

A consultancy will expect to respond to a pitch by writing a proposal and then presenting this to you and your senior colleagues. It's up to you how formal you wish the presentation to be – you could demand a full, stand up presentation or simply ask the agency to return to present their ideas less formally within the context of a meeting. There are no fixed rules, but the more formal the occasion the more serious the atmosphere, and usually the larger the budget.

Don't expect the presentation, or the accompanying document, to deliver a fully detailed breakdown of the activities your proposed campaign will comprise. These ideas are the consultancy's 'product' and they are understandably reluctant to give them away for free. In fact, if you want a fully detailed campaign plan then some agencies may demand a fee for drawing one up. This is not so difficult to understand when you consider how much time it could take to create a presentation, and that there is nothing to prevent you from refusing to employ the agency but using their ideas anyway.

You want to gain a good idea of the approach the consultancy would take when handling your account: the type of activities it would recommend; the team which would be working with you; and their response to any specific issues raised in the brief. Overall, you want to know that all the points raised at the briefing stage have been addressed, and to be able to judge whether or not the agency has fully understood the nature of your organization and the context in which it operates. You'll also expect to hear reasons why the consultancy thinks it is ideally suited to handling your account, and to gain a fuller picture of the way in which the agency operates – its company history, its current and past client list, its specialities, and the credentials of the proposed account team. This meeting is also a chance for you and your colleagues to ask lots of questions, so make sure you make the most of the opportunity.

Confirming the appointment

Try to keep your final decision time down to an absolute minimum. Not only will it be easier to make a judgement when impressions are still fresh, but it is also fairer on the consultancies you have asked to pitch. Once you have made your decision, then you need to formally appoint the consultancy of your choice – and let the others know that they were unsuccessful. If they ask for feedback do provide it – it's often very useful for an agency to know the reasons why they didn't get the business, especially if they thought that their presentation went well.

You'll now move into the realms of formal contracts and signed agreements. Make sure a review period is included – if things do not go as well as you hoped, then you may wish to run the whole exercise again, possibly inviting the current incumbent to re-pitch against those less successful last time around.

Finding an independent consultant

Although freelance PR advisers abound, finding them can prove remarkably difficult. A single person does not need a lot of business in order to fill up their time completely, and, of course, the good ones will always be busy and will not need to advertise, whilst those with plenty of time to spare may either be inexperienced, starting out or simply not very good!

Finding an independent consultant is, in fact, a very similar process to finding an agency. Professional bodies and advisers can prove a useful source of information, but word of mouth is also invaluable. Many advisers work with designers and through other marketing agencies, so that is a good place to start, as well as asking other marketing managers you may know. Local business advisers are often aware of local independents, and some business advice services run contact databases which can provide useful leads. Specialist recruitment agencies also exist which can help you find a freelance, but of course that would be for a fee. You could even advertise in your local paper, as this would also provide a list of good alternatives, useful if your first choice proves unsuccessful, or if you find the workload is too much for one person to handle.

Once you have found a likely freelance, invite them in for an initial meeting, and ask to see their portfolio and to hear about other work they have been or are currently doing. Once again, chemistry is all-important, and it's often the case that you will feel happy enough by the end of this initial meeting to start a few projects rolling – alternatively, you can ask them to complete a trial project in order to judge the quality of the work they do and the way in which they do it. Overall, the relationship will be much less formal than that with a consultancy, and you can easily establish whether you want to work on a project-by-project basis or by arranging a regular monthly commitment. This latter arrangement does depend upon you being able to generate enough work for the freelance to do, but gives you the advantage of knowing that you have a resource in place, and also gives the freelance a certain assurance that those hours reserved for your organization will be used, and that any other offers of work can be safely turned down.

Appointing an in-house PRO

The basic procedure for this will reflect the HR protocols you have already in place for your organization. As outlined on page 150, you must decide the level at which you want your PRO to operate, and whether you are happy to appoint someone who will need training or would rather hire proven skills and expertise up front. Whatever the level of appointment you decide to make, ensure that the person you choose for the job already has good writing skills, is a good administrator and is 'media aware' – or at least has the potential to acquire these attributes. Although experience of your industry sector would be an advantage, a general all-round knowledge of PR is more valuable.

Managing your professional PR resource

Employing dedicated PR help does not mean that you can forget about PR. In fact, you may find yourself being even more actively involved than before, although hopefully at a more executive level. Your input will still be vital at a number of different levels:

Regular strategic input

You must be prepared to devote regular time to the PR programme at the strategic level. PR administration usually focuses on a regular meeting, usually monthly, with additional meetings as necessary to concentrate on particular issues or activities. At this main meeting, you want to gain an overview of ongoing progress, identify any problem areas and help identify new directions in which activities could move – although you can expect your team to advise you on strategy and tactics, you will still be required to provide the fundamental steer which will ensure that the programme remains on track. You need to let your team know of any new developments – both internal and external – which may affect the way your PR campaign progresses, as only you can judge the potential importance of these developments and advise on the level of response required.

Approval of PR material

Most PR activities result in the production of written material destined to appear in the public domain – whether in the media, online, or as a piece of corporate literature. It's very important therefore, that nothing is issued which does not have the full approval of a senior manager, as well as the approval of any third parties that may have been mentioned in the text (see page 67 for more on this). A fully documented, agreed approval process is fundamental to the whole PR process but depends entirely upon your availability to read and approve the material produced. If you know that you will not always be able to turn material around fast enough – especially when deadlines are tight – then name other colleagues who can act on your behalf.

As a spokesperson

Ideally your team does not want to speak for you, although they often have to in the course of their work. Their aim is to act as an interface between you and your audiences: when actual comment is required, or expert information sought, then you should be the one to provide the answers. Be prepared, therefore, to speak on behalf of your organization whenever necessary – from providing a journalist with background information for a press release, to introducing or giving a seminar. If you know that your availability may be limited, name colleagues who can step into this role. If you have put together a Media Guide (see page 44) then you will already have a list of experts, but you will have to provide additional guidance on who can be trusted to speak on behalf of the organization as a whole. Your crisis management strategy (see page 128) will also have produced a list of approved spokespeople.

As a judge of opportunities

Not all PR opportunities can wait until a scheduled meeting in order to be actioned – and an active PR team will constantly be on the lookout for opportunities which could work in your favour. Once again, although your PRO can advise on the merits or otherwise of taking advantage of an unexpected opportunity, they will still need access to a senior manager in order to get the go ahead – especially if the decision has a budgetary implication.

To evaluate ongoing performance

You are the ultimate manager of the PR strategy and need to be aware of its progress and to evaluate its success or otherwise. You also need to assess the effectiveness of your team or your consultants. We'll be looking at evaluation in more detail in the next chapter, but it's important to note here that effective evaluation still remains your responsibility.

Exercise

What is the ideal PR team profile for the following organizations?:

- An SMO planning a limited campaign comprising mainly 'high-level', highly targeted activities.
- A large company planning an international consumer campaign, starting with a major product launch.
- A local information service running a number of small-scale activities targeted at a variety of audiences, needing to repeat the same messages in a number of different ways.

11 | EVALUATING SUCCESS

A common criticism of Public Relations is that it is difficult to evaluate effectively, and it's easy to see why. PR is often implemented in order to achieve goals such as 'raising awareness', or 'enhancing relations with key groups'. Although these are valid aims, they are often couched in such nebulous terms that it is difficult to imagine how to start to measure such concepts as awareness. But nevertheless, effective evaluation is vital – otherwise, how can you be sure that your programme is achieving its overall objectives, and that your budget is being wisely spent?

Setting measurable aims and objectives

In order to set some parameters for your evaluation process, it's important to revisit the aims and objectives of your PR programme – and to recap, we defined aims as your overarching goals, and objectives as the practical means by which you will achieve these goals. It is the objectives which are translated into tangible PR activities.

If you want to evaluate something, then you need to be able to assess it in the context of a *measurable* aim or objective. If you can't measure it, in some form or other (and we'll look at how to define this term in more detail shortly), then how can you tell if you've achieved it? It's also crucial that these aims and objectives are realistic – both in terms of the nature of your organization, and the level of success you can realistically hope to achieve, at least within the timeframe of your evaluation period. You may want to appear on the front page of the *Financial Times*, for example, but in reality, is it ever going to happen? Perhaps if your organization suddenly becomes incredibly newsworthy (and this may be for negative as well as positive reasons) then it may occur, but if not then don't expect PR to achieve miracles.

Let's look at some examples, and identify the ways in which an aim can be evaluated with some degree of rigour – and then we'll look more closely at practical evaluation activities to see how they work.

For the purposes of this exercise we have been deliberately simplistic – each of the aims listed below could well be translated into a broader range of objectives, but at least they give some idea of how to begin the process:

Aim	Objective	Evaluation
To become known by consumers as a leading supplier of Produce X.	To gain increased coverage within identified consumer media.	Monitor and evaluate press coverage within identified consumer media.
To raise the profile of our organization among financial directors of blue chip companies.	To produce a discursive newsletter, addressing issues of interest and relevance.	Use a high quality mailing list to ensure newsletter is received by right people; analyse feedback mechanisms incorporated into newsletter.
To make local business advisers aware of service X, and of the benefits it could offer their clients.	Hold a launch event designed specifically to attract that audience, backed by a targeted media and promotional campaign.	Use a targeted mailing list to ensure the information is received by all members of target group; analyse profile of guests attending event; analyse media coverage.

However, before you begin to evaluate, it's also important to keep in mind the context within which your PR campaign has been operating, as this also has an impact upon the end result. For example, you may consider the budget for your PR campaign to be very generous, but how does it compare to your advertising spend, or your exhibition budget? If you are expecting to identify a direct contribution to the bottom line, then make sure it's along the same percentages as your budget division. Also make sure that any analysis takes notice of other marketing activities taking place at the same time. If you are concentrating solely on PR, then it's easier to assess its impact – if you are also running major direct mail and advertising campaigns, then your target groups will be exposed to information from a variety of sources, and you may need to weight your final evaluation accordingly.

Evaluation techniques

Now let's look at some different types of evaluation techniques, so that you can identify the most appropriate to your own strategy.

Awareness surveys

If 'raising general awareness' is one of your central aims, and you really want to get an accurate assessment of how well your programme has performed, then a two-stage awareness survey is the only real way of achieving this – but unfortunately probably the most expensive. In brief, you must survey your target audiences prior to the launch of your PR campaign, or before a major activity such as a sponsorship or new product launch, and establish levels of awareness – for example, the level of familiarity with your name or brand, a rating against competitor products or organizations, and an awareness of other related issues if pertinent. The PR campaign is then launched, runs for a predetermined period, and the survey is then repeated. A comparison of results will show if your PR strategy has resulted in a significant increase in awareness amongst your target audience. An awareness survey differs from a communications audit (see page 121) primarily in its aims – you want to establish levels of awareness, not the means by which it was generated.

This is an expensive exercise, and so only really relevant if your proposed PR spend is significant, and your target audience large enough to survey effectively – major brands, household names, large corporations use this technique on a regular basis because they need to be highly sensitive to changes in the marketplace, but if you are a small or medium organization, and if your brand or product range is well defined, then such an exercise is unnecessary. Alternatively, if you don't want, or can't afford to question large numbers of individuals, then using focus groups for more in-depth analysis could be another option.

Another route is to take part in an 'omnibus' survey – many commercial research firms run surveys on behalf of a number of organizations. You only pay a percentage of the cost of the entire exercise, and only get to ask a few questions, but at least your target groups are being surveyed. Even cheaper, is to simply buy the results of one of the major market surveys that are constantly on offer, and pick and choose amongst the information provided in order to establish a base level for your own particular campaign.

Evaluating media liaison campaigns

As media liaison is often such an important element within a campaign, it's important that is evaluated as thoroughly as possible, and there are a number of distinct activities which you could undertake:

Monitoring coverage

One of the best and most obvious ways of assessing the success of your media liaison programme (and, by default, the relevance of the information that you are sending to the media), is to monitor, record and analyse all media coverage you gain. If your programme is operating on a small scale, and your press list is very limited, then you may be able to handle this in-house – you know who is receiving your press releases, so simply read, watch or listen to those media and record the instances when your name appears. If national newspapers are included in your press list, then make sure you register with the Newspaper Licensing Agency (NLA) – this was established in 1996 to enable organizations to lawfully copy newspaper press cuttings for internal management purposes.

Full details of how to register and obtain a licence, plus lists of the publications which come under this regulation, can be found at the NLA's web site.

However, it doesn't take long for even a modest media campaign to start to generate results, and for your organization to receive wider coverage than originally expected, and so if you want to get a better picture of who is using your press information then it's time to get professional help – for example:

Cuttings agencies

A number of well-known, long-established press cuttings agencies exist and you can find contact details in trade directories, Yellow Pages or within PR industry magazines. Whichever agency you use, make sure it is registered with the NLA. Agencies employ scores of people to read all manner of publications and to then cut and paste any cuttings they find. Reading lists are usually divided into trade or consumer press, and you are charged according to the list you select – of course, you can have both if necessary. You must also identify key words – usually the name of your organization, or a particular product – on which the reader will cut. A reading fee is then charged, plus an additional fee per cutting. Cuttings agencies are not perfect – they cannot guarantee complete success, but they do undertake a regular sweep of your target press. Most will ask you to copy press releases and distribution lists to them, so their readers can be primed, but they will also highlight those occasions where your name has been mentioned without your knowledge, and these can provide an important measure of how well your reputation is spreading. You can also ask the agency to cut on other words, if you feel you need to instigate a 'current awareness' survey, even if it's only for a limited period. You could then assess the press coverage given to a certain issue, technology, or even to rival organizations.

Media monitoring services

If you are planning to achieve TV, internet or radio coverage then you will also want a record of those instances when your organization was featured. Once again agencies exist which will do this for you, and can advise you of any copyright implications. If you know which programme is likely to feature your organization then it will be easy enough to instruct the agency as to which programme to monitor, but if you've sent out a video release, or syndicated a taped interview, then be prepared to pay more if they have to scan all likely programmes in order to catch any coverage you may generate. If you have used a media services agency to prepare and distribute a tape for you, then subsequent monitoring is often included as part of the total package.

Assessing the value of media coverage

If you want to assess the *value* of the coverage you've gained, then a numerical count of column centimetres or broadcast seconds – although often gratifying – is not enough. You need to look more closely at the type of coverage you've received, and the benefits you've gained from it. Specialist software does exist which can provide an ongoing analysis of coverage as it is received, but such systems are really only useful if you generate regular coverage and a constant assessment of its quality is vital to your work.

If you simply want to evaluate a relatively modest media campaign, then consider the following criteria when looking at every instance of coverage gained:

- **Vehicle:** Was the coverage gained in one of your main target media?
- **Placement:** When analysing press cuttings, consider issues such as the section in which it was featured, its position within the running order (nicely up front or buried at the back?) and even its position on the page – was it on the right-hand side (guaranteed to achieve a higher number of readers), placed near main editorial, stuck on a left-hand page, or hidden away at the back among the small ads? Likewise, did your news make the headlines on the radio or TV programme which featured it, or was it used for light relief – or worse, were you filmed or recorded and then not featured at all?

- **Presentation:** Was a photo used (and did you have to pay for it?); what was the headline; was the whole press release used or just the first paragraph (or less)?
- **Quality:** Is the copy accurate? If you are mentioned within a broader news story or other analytical feature, is your organization given positive, neutral or negative coverage? Were you quoted verbatim, edited or – worse – misquoted?
- **Positive or negative?:** If coverage was not simply factual, was it positive or negative? If negative, why?
- **Competition:** Did anything steal the limelight just when you were hoping to make a major splash (is it worth, in fact, reissuing the news again if it was smothered by a story which broke unexpectedly)? Did similar news from rival organizations gain better exposure than your own? Can you tell why?
- **Feedback:** How was your organization credited? Have you been able to directly attribute any response to the coverage you received (see 'feedback mechanisms', later on in this chapter, for more about this)? And don't forget the quality of the feedback – you may be getting a lot of enquiries but are they from your key target groups? And if not, why not?
- **Unsolicited coverage:** How much of coverage was unsolicited – perhaps you were mentioned in the context of another article or your MD was quoted in a news report. Is this increasing or not? Is the coverage received in this way positive or negative? How many of the unsolicited calls that you've received from journalists have turned into valuable coverage?

You also need to identify, in due course, the media which did not feature your news, by logging coverage against your original distribution list. Don't start this review too quickly – if your news was not time critical (a contract announcement for example) then a publication may well hold it back until the next edition. You may find that some press releases are still generating coverage even months after you originally dispatched them. If you find that your news is rarely being covered, then review your press release style and your distribution list – perhaps your news simply isn't relevant for the media you've identified. Perhaps you're being too ambitious. Perhaps you're not supplying the type of information the magazine or programme wants to receive. You'll probably find that the 'B' list media are those which rarely cover your news, so you can also use this as a cleaning exercise, honing down your list to those media you know are showing a sustained interest, and reserving the other titles and programmes for those occasions when you have something more relevant to say.

Representative value

Although this is a rather controversial method of assessment – and not one actively encouraged by the PR profession – another means of assessing coverage is to calculate its equivalent value in terms of advertising spend. Of course, the result will not reflect the quality of the coverage received, but if budgets are under discussion it can be at least one way of demonstrating the value of a media liaison campaign. You'll be able to obtain advertising rates from a magazine or broadcaster's advertising department, and you simply have to evaluate like for like. Rates will vary tremendously from one publication to the next, so you'll have to do this exercise very specifically, taking into account variables such as the size and placement of the cutting, whether a colour or black and white photo was used and where the cutting appeared in relation to the main editorial.

So, just when you thought that gaining press coverage was enough of an achievement in itself, you now realize how much more you have to think about! As you can imagine, for major multinational organizations, the monitoring and analysis of media coverage becomes an all-important routine which goes on around the clock. But in reality, the results of a modest media liaison campaign will be relatively easy to assess – you'll know the value of the magazines or programmes in which you were featured, and already have a fair idea of the sections in which your releases are most likely to gain coverage. But nevertheless, it's worth having these assessment criteria in the back of your mind as you look over the coverage you've received. You need to be sure that the type of coverage you are generating reflects the quality of the information you are putting out, and if not why not?

Analysis of direct feedback

Wherever possible, include a 'feedback mechanism' within every PR activity – use your judgement to decide how overt you want this to be, depending upon the nature of the vehicle or activity you are implementing. The results will provide you with the raw data essential to a full understanding of the success or otherwise of the exercise you undertook. For example, here are some feedback mechanisms relating to specific activities:

Material issued to the media

Always make sure that address and contact details are included at the bottom of every press release of other information. Although it's rare that these will be reproduced verbatim, most trade publications operate a referral service in which reader enquiries (usually ticked on a 'bingo card' inserted into the magazine in question) are processed and names and addresses forwarded to the relevant organizations which have been featured. Always make reference to your web site (assuming you have one) as this provides a useful direct link.

Record any feedback which can be attributed directly to specific coverage – you'll already be recording any contact you've had from journalists, but you also need to analyse direct requests for brochures and other information. Although this can sometimes prove difficult when relating calls directly to press coverage, if you've been running a competition or giveaway offer it will be simple to analyse the number of responses you received.

Events

A delegate questionnaire can be used to generate instant feedback from almost any type of event. It's best not to make such forms too long or difficult – if your delegates don't hand them back at the end of the event then it's unlikely they will remember to do so later – and use multiple choice questions as much as possible. Incentives, such as entry into a prize draw, can also encourage an increased return, but only use this device if you feel it fits in with the tone of the occasion. As well as including such questionnaires in delegate packs, you can also hand them out to guests as they leave, or post or e.mail them on afterwards.

Newsletters, and other literature

It seems obvious but don't forget to put contact details on all literature, especially those items produced within your PR campaign. Newsletters provide an ideal opportunity to include more specific contacts – sales directors, representatives etc., who may be of interest to your target audiences. As we discussed in Chapter 4, the infrequent inclusion of a questionnaire can also be used to gain more detailed information. A direct incentive (a bribe in other words) to return the questionnaire will certainly up your return rate, and may be considered a worthwhile investment if you really want to find out the views of your readership.

Make sure your web site gets plenty of mentions as well – directing as much traffic as possible onto a well-designed web site can deliver significant added value, and can once again help provide a valuable filter.

Track requests for all types of literature and wherever possible match against specific PR activities to see if you can identify any positive effects.

Web sites

Regular monitoring of hits will indicate how well your overall promotional campaign is progressing, but if the hit rate increases directly after a specific PR push, or after a particularly valuable piece of press coverage, then you can confidently use this as positive evidence. Once again, however, the quality of contact is important – it's not enough just to know that more people have visited your site, but are they of the right quality, or of direct relevance? The response gained from information request forms or e.mail queries should provide some answers.

Sponsorships

See Chapter 5 for more on the specific evaluation of Sponsorship activities.

Indirect feedback

As your PR campaign progresses, you should also begin to get a 'feel' for how well things are going simply as a result of the daily conversations you have with your target audiences. Start to make a note of any interesting comments such as 'we saw you in the paper the other day', try to evaluate how familiar your name has become. It may seem all rather nebulous, but gut feeling does play a role in the whole process and so shouldn't be ignored.

Canvass other sections within your organization to see if they are handling more enquiries, or have received more positive feedback from existing customers, or from suppliers or other contacts. It can all help you gather together evidence to indicate whether or not your PR plan is on the right track.

Dealing with success

It's one thing to run a successful PR campaign and to generate lots of leads, but you then have to capitalize upon this interest. If your sales and marketing teams are unable to convert quality leads into promising sales contacts then all your hard work will be undone, and it's important to remember this when analysing the effectiveness of the strategy as a whole, especially its contribution to bottom line. It's also important to back fine words with concrete actions. As we noted in Chapter 7, one of the most common grievances noted by staff when it comes to considering the matter of corporate communications is that a company will say one thing whilst doing the opposite. Once you have started to establish a clearer image in the public eye, it's important that you strive to live up to that image or else run the risk of undermining all the good that your programme has achieved on your behalf.

Staff response

We've already noted the importance of keeping your staff, your sales team, distributors or representatives informed of your PR programme. They need to know – ahead of time – if a press release is about to be issued, so that they can be prepared for increase in interest, and can talk knowledgeably about any press coverage that has been received. This is particularly important if you expect to generate a lot of publicity at once – a product launch for example, or the announcement of a new service or technology. We've all read about companies who have been unable to keep up with the demand that their promotional activities have generated and as a result, ironically, generating much negative PR. Of course, you need to judge exactly which staff should know what, but whatever you decide to tell them, anything is better than nothing.

Evaluation – how often?

How often should you evaluate your PR campaign? Although this does depend greatly upon the mix of activities you've chosen to implement, evaluation should be carried out regularly, in order to ensure that the programme remains on track, and also – over the longer term – in order to identify any positive trends that could be exploited, or negative trends that should be investigated. Make evaluation a stock item on the agenda of your regular PR meeting: look at issues such as media coverage, journalists contact and review any feedback from specific events. Depending upon the extent of your programme, also aim to undertake a more in-depth review either six-monthly or annually. Aim to assess the contribution of each element within the programme and try to identify areas of concern, areas of success and directions in which to move forward.

Evaluation is a crucial element of the next stage of your PR programme – planning next year's strategy – so good luck!

Exercise

Which evaluation mechanisms would you employ in order to assess:

■ A Christmas party for business contacts?
■ A seminar?
■ A syndicated competition?
■ A trade press release?

PR Matrix

Time to complete the Matrix. You'll now need to add a final column, Evaluation, and for each activity that you've identified, list precisely the terms by which you'll evaluate its success.

Now all you need to do is put the whole programme into action!

USEFUL ADDRESSES

The Institute of Public Relations (IPR)

The Old Trading House
15 Northburgh Street
London EC1V OPR
United Kingdom
Tel: 020 7253 5151
Fax: 020 7490 0588
www.ipr.org.uk

Public Relations Consultants Association (PRCA)

Willow House
Willow Place
Victoria
London SW1P 1JH
United Kingdom
Tel: 020 7233 6026
Fax: 020 7828 4797
www.prca.org.uk

Newspaper Licensing Agency (NLA)

Tunbridge Wells
Kent TN1 1NL
United Kingdom
Tel: 01892 525274
Fax: 01892 525275
www.nla.co.uk

PR Week

174 Hammersmith Road
London W6 7JP
United Kingdom
Tel: 020 8267 4429
Fax: 020 8267 4509
www.prweek.com

INDEX

TEACH YOURSELF

BUSINESS PRESENTATIONS

Angela Murray

Giving a presentation can be a daunting and nerve-racking experience, even for a regular presenter – what can you do to give yourself confidence and ensure success? *Teach Yourself Business Presentations* provides the answer. From defining the brief to post-presentation analysis, the book supplies a step-by-step guide to the skills and techniques needed to deliver an effective, engaging presentation.

Team presentations, presentations to colleagues, informative and persuasive presentations – appropriate techniques are considered for these and many more. Throughout the book imagination, innovation and creativity are all actively encouraged.

Covered in the book:

- strategic planning – defining and analysing a brief
- planning and research
- creativity
- communication skills
- audio-visual aids
- 'presentation etiquette' and personal presentation
- analysing performance.

An easy-to-read guide, full of hints and tips, this book provides support and guidance for the novice, and fresh ideas for the more experienced.

Angela Murray is a freelance Business Consultant in marketing communications and presentation skills.

TEACH YOURSELF

NEGOTIATING

Phil Baguley

Teach Yourself Negotiating is an important book for all professionals. The need to negotiate effectively exists at all levels in all organizations. Whether you are dealing with colleagues, suppliers or customers you need to be able to negotiate – and do it well.

A book you cannot afford to be without, *Teach Yourself Negotiating*:

- shows you how to prepare for, carry out and complete your negotiations
- helps you decide what strategies and tactics to use
- illustrates how to use the bargaining process to generate a successful outcome
- guides you to a successful implementation of that outcome
- provides a checklist for assessing your own negotiating skills.

Phil Baguley is an experienced business writer and lecturer. He has held senior management roles in multinational corporations and has also worked as a management consultant in the UK and Europe. He is also the author of *Teach Yourself Project Management* and *Teach Yourself Surviving Your Organization*.

TEACH YOURSELF

PERFORMANCE APPRAISALS

Polly Bird

All managers have to carry out staff appraisals, and *Teach Yourself Performance Appraisals* provides the guidelines and help on how to do this effectively and obtain the desired results. The book deals with each stage of appraising, from preparation to evaluation. It also gives advice on how to cope with difficulties during the appraisal process, as well as how to handle your own appraisal.

The book is written in a practical and straightforward way and includes:

- guidance to managers new to appraisals, and those who want to improve
- advice on how to turn discussion into action
- help with upward appraisals.

Polly Bird is a professional writer of business and training books.